The Unrated Colors of Guatemala

Fabian Hernandez

Dedication

To my brothers… Mario, Ervin, and Geo.

Thanks for always inspiring me, each in your own unique way.
Love you, guys.

Fiction is everywhere you look.

Contents

Chapter One
Guatemala City

May 26, 2010

The weekend had finally arrived. Jorge walked out the doors of the bank where he worked as a junior analyst. He walked with a sense of urgency as though a fire was burning in his soul, and he needed to release the energy, someway, somehow. He got into his car with the urge to drive far away from the realities that burdened his thoughts.

Jorge wanted a new adventure, one that could rejuvenate his spirit and help take away the pain in his gut. He took out his iPod, connected it to the car radio, and set the classic rock playlist. He reached the back seat and grabbed his book bag, where his weed was stashed. He packed the bullet pipe and took the first hit since lunch, holding in the smoke, which gave the THC enough time to fully saturate his blood. When he exhaled, it was as though he was letting out every inner thought of the day, of the week, and of the last eight years. "Let's get the fuck out of here, Jorge," he said to himself before turning on the ignition and driving down La Petapa Avenue.

In the section of San Cristobal, a bus filled beyond capacity stopped to let a young man off. "San Cristobal! San Cristobal!" yelled the bus driver's assistant to alert all other passengers. Chavez stepped onto the road. He adjusted his hat, which covered his curly afro, and started walking home. He had faith in God that he would get there safely, but as he walked down San Cristobal Avenue, Chavez thought of all the danger that plagued his neighborhood and threatened the innocent.

San Cristobal lay outside the western border of Guatemala City. It was once considered an upper-class section of Guatemala in the seventies. Over the years, drug smugglers pushed cocaine into the capital, and San Cristobal became a watchtower for their operations. It became a volatile place for the people who continued to reside there.

On the way to his house, Chavez walked by a small eatery that sold chicken quesadillas for five quetzals. "Una quesadilla por favor," he politely asked the old woman cooking the food, who, in all likelihood, was the owner of the place. There was nothing fancy about the establishment. Chavez tried to find a place to sit, but the only seats available were old water barrels that were being occupied by a group of construction workers who were finishing their day with a round of beers.

He stood against a wall and picked up the local newspaper. The front page showed a picture of police investigating two dead bodies that were discovered in a ditch by the city of Mixco. The headline read, "Massacre Brutal en Mixco!" Chavez shook his head in disgust at the horrible image. "Always the same shit," he said to himself while turning the page in hopes of finding a more uplifting article, but there weren't any. Instead, he took a look at the classifieds to review the job openings. Chavez was desperate to find a job that paid more than his current one as an assistant at his father's warehouse. Without an education, his choices were limited. Every job that was listed required some degree of training or post-high school education, which he lacked. It gave him a hopeless feeling in regard to his future.

His phone vibrated as he put the paper away. It was a text

message from Edgar, his friend and drug dealer. The message read, in Spanish, [Do you still need that favor?] Chavez wanted to text him back, but his phone was out of minutes, and the only money he had left was to buy drugs. "Señor, su comida esta listo!" announced the old lady.

A few blocks away, the drug-dealing hippy named Edgar was inside the kitchen of his home cooking rice. Once there was a steady boil in the pot, he aimed his focus at the two pounds of weed sitting on the kitchen table. He sat down and lit a large joint before breaking up the weed into individual sandwich bags. He used an electronic scale to weigh out each bag to one-eighth of an ounce. Edgar sold each bag for sixty quetzals, which would gross him a thirty percent profit on each pound he bought.

Just as he was finishing the packing, the doorbell rang. He wasn't expecting anyone at the time, so it made him a little paranoid. Edgar put the weed into an old school bag and crept quietly to the front gate to see who it was. He couldn't hear anything, so he looked cautiously through the peephole and was relieved to see that it wasn't the police.

"Chavez," he said.

"Who the hell did you think it was? Your boyfriend?" responded Chavez as he entered the courtyard and slapped his hands with Edgar.

"Fuck you. I'm paranoid. A house down the street was raided by police last week, and to make things worse, Smiley has been looking for me," he said as he scoped the street before closing the door.

"Why would he be looking for you?" asked Chavez. He

wondered how this small-time dealer had business with a well-known criminal and murderer like Smiley.

"Never mind, my rice is cooking. Let's go inside," said Edgar.

It was Chavez's first time in the new place. Edgar moved around more often than most people; it was one of his characteristic traits for those who knew him. "The place looks good. It's a lot bigger than the last house you were staying at," said Chavez before sitting down on the edge of the couch that had a giant hole in the middle. It looked as though a shotgun had blown a hole through it. Chavez didn't want to be rude, so he didn't ask if that was what happened.

Chavez sat on the hard edge with his back straight and both arms balancing his weight on his thighs. He took a minute to admire the design of the living room. The small space was painted bright orange with a door entrance to the kitchen on one side and a hallway that led to the bedrooms on the other. He took special notice of the Bob Marley poster that hung at the other end of the room. Marley was Chavez's favorite artist. The only other furniture in sight was a recliner and an old, five-disc stereo that was set on the floor.

Edgar came out of the kitchen with his long hair in a ponytail, holding the book bag that was filled with weed. "What the fuck, Chavez? How's everything?" he asked with a smile. They'd known each other for nearly ten years, ever since the day Edgar moved to the neighborhood.

"Good, working for my old man... smoking," he chuckled. Chavez was a man of few words. He wasn't meek, only a little shy under normal circumstances, except when drunk.

Edgar sat on his recliner, which was perfectly placed in the center of the room, like a throne. "What was it you wanted?" he asked Chavez in a typical, calm fashion. Edgar placed his book bag on the floor and exposed his weed supply. Chavez was instantly distracted by the sight.

"A few hits of LSD," he replied. "Are these for Twisted Mushroom Fest tonight?" asked Edgar as he searched through his drug kit for the acid papers.

"You know it. I read the DJ list online, and it looks like a pretty good lineup. Paul Davila is going to be there," said Chavez.

"Do you have tickets?" asked Edgar, who was unable to find any at a reasonable price. "No, but I'm sure I'll get in, somehow," replied Chavez with confidence. "I was thinking about going too, but someone told me that security was going to be tight. And I can't afford a ticket at full price. Three fifty is too much," said Edgar with a look of regret on his face.

"Supposedly, there's a way in; at least, that's what Jorge told me," said Chavez to give Edgar hope.

"That Jorge, he's funny as shit. Last night, he came here drunk to buy weed and started to tell me about some high school girl that he's sleeping with," said Edgar.

Chavez laughed and said, "Yea, that crazy asshole can't keep it in his pants."

Edgar found the small paper acid hits and gave them to Chavez in a small plastic bag. "These are what I have. I took three the night I went to Atitlan, and they were strong." Chavez grabbed the plastic baggy from Edgar's hands and held it with his thumb and index finger.

"Are you sure they're good?" asked Chavez to confirm that he was buying something that would give him a strong trip.

"I'm telling you. You're going to see all sorts of visuals. A group of us went over to San Pedro and got a hotel room for the night. I took them around ten, and by midnight I had walked off on my own into the jungle. I heard all sorts of things, man. At some point, I thought a tree was trying to talk to me," said Edgar.

Chavez appreciated the warning and was eager to take them. He handed Edgar the money and stuck the drugs in his pocket.

Edgar pulled out and lit a joint. The marijuana was called Oaxaca. It was grown in San Pedro, a hidden pueblo on Lake Atitlan, where Edgar would go to restock his supply twice a month. "Here, try this. It's a new batch of Oaxaca," he said while passing the joint. Chavez was always in the mood to smoke, so he took some time to relax and enjoy the free weed.

He took a big hit and said in a parched voice while holding in the smoke, "It has a good taste. It's fresh." After a few more hits, Chavez became very comfortable. He suddenly started to think about Edgar's ties with a ruthless criminal like Smiley. By no means were he and Edgar best friends, but he still knew him enough to be concerned.

"So, why is Smiley looking for you?" he asked Edgar while taking another hit. Edgar was organizing his supplies in the book bag when he heard the name Smiley. His face froze. The idea that he was being sought by a soulless murderer like Smiley frightened him. "What happened was, last week, I went down to Devil's Factory to buy some heroin for a friend," said Edgar. Chavez was shocked that Edgar was crazy enough to go to such a place. He wondered if Edgar was buying the heroine for himself. "Shit, that's

16th Street Mafia territory. Are you crazy?" said Chavez. "I don't know, man. But I wish that I had never gone there. That place was a nightmare.

"Devil's Factory was well known for being the 16th Street Mafia's central base of drug distribution. Smiley was the leader of the gang and ran the entire operation with an iron fist. He'd once gone on record to a journalist saying that he was the devil's soldier and that it was his mission to make the world as black as his heart. All he knew was squalor and suffering, which enraged him. He never knew his mother or his father. He was raped as a child by unknown attackers and started doing drugs by the time he was six. Smiley committed his first murder at the age of nine and was in jail by the age of ten. His life had been a struggle for survival; through killing and stealing, he rose to form the 16th Street Mafia.

"Not even the police go in there. I heard that an entire family was gunned down because they got lost and were driving around with the windows up," added Chavez.

"Yeah, I heard about that. That's why I parked a few kilometers away, near the shopping center, and walked the rest of the way. There were junkies walking around everywhere like zombies. No lights work out there. I'm not going to lie. I was a little scared. I didn't know if someone was going to see me and either rob me or kill me," expressed Edgar.

"Once you get to the corner of 16th Street and 12th Avenue, there are guys with guns standing on the rooftops, watching every move you make. I went in with my hands up," said Edgar while raising his hands to animate what he was saying.

"Ahuevos," agreed Chavez while smoking the joint. He passed it back to Edgar.

Edgar continued. "There were all sorts of people doing drugs right there on the street. I saw a mother put her swaddled baby on the ground to shoot heroin in her arm. After I bought the drugs, I saw the same lady leaning over a table, and the baby was still lying on the street."

Chavez was in awe. "Shit, man, did you try helping it or something?" he asked Edgar.

"I didn't want to be the cause of any drama, not there," responded Edgar before holding the smoke in his lungs and then exhaling with great force. "But let me tell you, that distribution system is organized. I was impressed." Edgar momentarily paused his story to grab a hair clip sitting in an ashtray and use it to unclog the joint.

"What happened when they gave you the drugs?" asked Chavez.

"When you get to the dead end, there's a table with two guys. One walks around and pats you down. The other takes your order. I gave the guy my money, and he walked to a back door that had a small depository. That's where another guy took the cash and passed the heroine."

"Ah, shit! It's like the drive-thru at the bank," said Chavez.

"Exactly!" replied Edgar with bloodshot eyes.

Chavez was amazed that he could finally claim that he knew someone who was crazy enough to go there. "So, why is Smiley looking for you," he asked Edgar. "That's the fucked up part," said Edgar as his tone became more serious. "As I was walking out of that place, I found a big bag of coke lying on the street. I couldn't leave it there," he said with a big smile while shaking his head.

Just then, a gray-haired feline quietly crept into the room and jumped on the other side of the couch where Chavez was sitting. "When did you get a cat?" asked Chavez. "I found her in the garden the day I moved in. She was this small when I found her," said Edgar while holding his hands close together to give Chavez an idea of the kitten's size. "Now she's big and fat," he added.

Chavez quickly turned his attention back to the story; he didn't care for cats and asked, "So, how much coke was there?" Edgar got to one knee on the floor to insert a CD into the stereo. His mind briefly drifted into the thought of playing Pink Floyd to accompany the mellow high. He inserted the CD, returned to the couch, and said, "I'm not sure, but at least a few ounces. The bag had a small hole, and a little fell out. And since the roof guards couldn't see me anymore, I picked it up and ran off. I didn't know who it belonged to, but I knew how much it was worth," replied Edgar, who took a hit of the joint before remembering that he didn't turn off the stove. He got up frantically and ran to the kitchen, leaving Chavez alone with the joint. He seized the moment and took five long drags.

Edgar returned, saying, "Three days ago, my friend, Juano, the one who brought the Colombian models to Jorge's house that one night, told me that Smiley's bodyguards were asking for me and asked if I'd been selling coke lately." Chavez knew what that meant. Smi- ley wasn't the type of person to ask many questions. He wanted to find Edgar and kill him for taking his coke. "What did you do with it?" asked Chavez as he passed the burning roach back to his host.

"Nothing, yet," said Edgar as small thoughts of a devised plan roamed his mind.

The joint finished, and Chavez went home. Along the way, he

tried to remember how Edgar graduated from a local marijuana dealer to a hardcore heroin user. He noticed the junky markings on his arm that scarred up from using needles. Chavez started realizing that they weren't kids anymore. He wasn't a kid anymore. The speed of life had distanced him from a childhood that was good and healthy. Now, he was a man with no identity. Chavez wasn't in school like most people his age. It worried him that his life had no direction at twenty-two.

He walked off the boulevard and passed the security gate of his neighborhood, where the guard was sitting on his stool eating a sour mango. The older man acknowledged Chavez and nodded his head while saying, "Good afternoon." Chavez waived back and continued walking. He turned the corner and noticed Jorge's car parked in front of his house.

Over in Guatemala's exclusive district, zone fourteen, Thomas Flores arrived home to his high-rise apartment. He was a Guatemalan/American who moved to Guatemala to attend dental school. After double majoring in Biology and Philosophy, he wasn't accepted to a single school in the United States. His grade point average wasn't high enough, and his entrance exam scores were average. Still, the persistent dreams of his father motivated him to continue forward. He moved to Guatemala in order to give dentistry a final try. He had no idea that the journey was destined to be for something greater.

The telephone was ringing as he walked into room 504. He placed his dental materials box on the floor and answered it.

"What the fuck, Flores?" It was Jorge. "I'm here with Chavez. We'll be over to pick you up around five." A night out drinking was exactly what he needed. Thomas wanted to blur his mind and forget about the fact that he was struggling in school.

"Sounds good. I'll see you then," he said to Jorge before hanging up the phone.

Still standing near the front entrance of the condo, Thomas looked at himself in the old, decorative mirror that belonged to the landlord and noticed how tired his eyes were. He focused deep into his pupils and said to himself, "What the hell are you doing, man?" He was exhausted from studying for final exams. It was just part of the reason that his mind wasn't as focused as it used to be. He felt that he wasn't the same uplifting young man that he once was. Guatemala had done something to his spirit. It had gradually taken away any remaining innocence he had before arriving.

Thomas sat on his couch to review the semester's final grades that had been posted online. While the web page was loading, he stared at a framed picture on the coffee table of him being held by his grandfather. Thomas didn't remember the day; he was only two years old when it was taken. The photo brought him a brief sense of joy.

The grades were displayed on the screen. There were no surprises. He'd passed all his courses, but his average score was just below 70%. If he received anything lower than 85% on the last exam, he would be suspended for a year. Thomas stared at the screen and wondered if the professors were deducting points because of wrong answers, grammatical errors, or bias. It was impossible to know because the exams weren't returned to the students. His neck tensed, and he started to bite his nails as he reviewed his last exam in his head. His Pharmacology score was the worst at 64 percent.

Regardless of how much he studied, he knew the language

barrier was affecting his grades dramatically. "Fucking Spanish," he said.

He lay down on the couch, rubbed his eyes, and said, "Why the fuck did I come here?" He looked at the picture of his grandfather a second time and felt hollow. He often had to remind himself that it was a rational choice to continue studying while his grandfather gradually faded away into the dark with a chronic kidney illness. At the time, Thomas thought he had done right by staying in Guatemala to finish the semester instead of flying home to be with his grandfather before he died. A tear seeped from his eye and down his cheek, feeling the guilt squeeze his heart. He wiped his face off with his arm and said, "Get a hold of yourself."

The mental exhaustion led him to empty out the tobacco from a cigar and replace it with weed to create a blunt. He lit it and lay back on the couch to stare out the window. The living room window spanned the entire west wall and looked out to the green mountain range in front. The apartment view was beautiful; it was where the land met the sky. Thomas smoked the entire blunt, methodically letting it run down until there was only a small roach left. A comfortable numbness had taken over his body, running through his blood and calming his thoughts.

Thomas was just closing his eyes when he heard the sound of his reggae ringtone. It was Mercedes Ibanez. She was the sixteen-year-old daughter of a family friend. The Ibanez family and the Flores family were more like family than friends.

"Hi, how are you?" she asked in an angelic tone.

"Good, you?" he replied. The two were nine years apart, but they had an unexplainable connection ever since she was little.

"Fine, I'm here in my room. What are you doing tonight?" she asked in her tiny girl voice. Mercedes would make it a point to ask him things in a particular manner to get his full attention. "I was thinking about going to dinner with a friend or maybe to a music festival," replied Thomas as he inspected an amalgam preparation on a plastic tooth he used to practice for his practical exam.

"Who are you going to dinner with? Another one of your sluts?" she asked. Thomas laughed at her jealousy. He thought it was adorable.

"Yeah, you know me. I need someone to pass the time with. It's not like I can spend my evening with you. As of late, every time I go over, you're busy talking with that guy." He was referring to a young college student who had been hanging around her house a little too often.

"Well, I don't talk to him anymore. Why don't you come over and we'll watch a movie tonight. Besides, there's something I need to tell you," she replied.

Thomas was her support through the blind years of high school. If she needed to talk to someone about anything, she would always go to him first.

"What's wrong? Are you okay?" asked Thomas out of concern for her mood.

"It's just that I'm having one of my bad days," she said. Thomas knew what that meant. Mercedes carried a giant void in her soul, and he was the only person that could help her get through the bad days. Thomas could hear her crying.

"What's wrong?" he asked again to get more insight into her pain.

"I just don't know, Thomas. No matter what I do or where I'm at, I'm always unhappy. I'm always crying when no one is looking, and I don't know how much longer I can go on living this way," she said to him.

Thomas knew how easily she could manipulate him into doing whatever she asked. He wanted to drive to her house to be with her, but he'd been trying to distance himself from Mercedes for quite some time.

"I'll let you know if my plans change. If not, I'll be over on Sunday, and we'll spend the day together, I promise," he said.

"Don't make promises you can't keep," replied Mercedes. She paused for a second in frustration and then continued by saying, "That's why I get mad at you. Every time I need to talk to you about something, you abandon me for your friends just to go get drunk," she said. Mercedes knew that a guilt trip always worked on Thomas, but not this time. As much as he loved seeing her face, he needed to deal with his problems with a solid night of partying.

"Don't get mad at me; the last few times I was over, you blew me off for your friends. I'll let you know what I do," said Thomas as he walked around his apartment looking for the dark blue jeans that fit his thirty-two-inch waist so well.

"Okay, let me know what you do," replied Mercedes. They agreed to talk later and said goodbye.

Thomas walked to the bathroom to take a shower. After drying himself, he noticed that the bristles on his toothbrush were left face down in the mildew that surrounded the sink. His knowledge of microorganisms caused him to grab a bottle of witch hazel, pour some into the cap, and leave the bristles soaking as he trimmed his beard stubble. He applied cologne, deodorant, and moisturizer. He was vain and liked looking good and being comfortable. He stared down at his toothbrush and determined that it was disinfected. He cleaned his entire mouth, palate, tongue, gums, and teeth. Thomas gave himself a look in the mirror, rubbed his hand through his buzzed haircut, and went to get dressed.

After putting on jeans, a white t-shirt, and a black, hooded, zip-up sweater, Thomas heard the security monitor ring. Maxwell, the security guard, was on the line for him. "Jorge Palma here to see you." Jorge was a regular at the condo. He'd become Thomas' closest friend in Guatemala. Jorge was the first person that Thomas ever had to learn to trust. They both yearned for something more than they currently had.

Jorge entered the apartment; his body tensed like a coiled wire. Chavez was humble as usual. Part of Jorge's uneasiness was due to the political scandal that had recently plagued the nation and further crippled the republic's trust in its government.

"What the fuck, Jorge? Did you see the video?" asked Thomas.

"Yeah, at work," replied Jorge. He sat down on the couch and gathered his thoughts before speaking. "I saw it too, but there were a few things that I didn't understand. Was he blaming the president for his murder or for all the crime that's happening in Guatemala?" asked Thomas.

"The president and his closest associates were accused of murder, drug trafficking, and embezzlement by a lawyer who was killed last Sunday, not too far from here. He left behind a video that was posted on the Internet an hour after the murder by one of his employees," replied Jorge. "I saw a large protest on my way to work this morning. They were blocking traffic, and a bus almost ran a group of people over while trying to get through," said Chavez.

"Yeah, I saw the same thing this morning on La Re- forma on my way to school. It looked like there were two different protests taking place side by side," said Thomas.

"That's what was happening. Over the week, the president spoke at a rally somewhere in Petén and got all the indigenous on his side by bribing them. He must have given them money and food. A lot of them are organizing their own protests in favor of the presidents' innocence," said Jorge as he took his pipe out of his pocket and placed it next to a micro motor that Thomas used for drilling plastic teeth.

"How was he killed? I've been so busy studying that I haven't had time to watch the news," said Thomas.

"He was riding his bike, and a truck ran him over. Supposedly, three men got out and then shot him a bunch of times in the face," said Chavez.

"The shit was a revelation from the grave. Rosenberg was a lawyer who was hired by a man named Daniel Santos, who was being charged unlawful property taxes on the prestigious farmland he owned in Petén. The land was bought from Fernando Soto, owner of the largest bank in Guatemala. Eventually, his bank seized the property, and Mr. Santos took the case into litigation with the help of Rosenberg," said Jorge.

"So that's when things started getting worse, right?" asked Thomas.

"That's what Rosenberg said. He said that Santos was threatened a few times and that his actions were angering people who didn't like inconveniences in their business practices. The bank offered to return his deposit and terminate the deal, but Santos didn't want that," said Jorge.

"He should have taken the money back. He would still be alive," said Thomas.

"He said that one Sunday morning, Mr. Santos took his teenage daughter out for breakfast on their usual weekend routine. On the way to the restaurant, two cars blocked Mr. Santos' truck into a street corner, and three men stepped out with guns. They pulled Mr. Santos and his daughter out of the truck and shot them both in the head. There were a bunch of witnesses. Nobody wants to say anything," explained Jorge.

"So why is the president involved?" asked Thomas. "Rosenberg wanted justice. He found out that Guatemala's Hydrocarbon Director advised President Colom that nearly three million barrels of crude oil had been discovered in Petén. Rosenberg uncovered signed documents from Vice President Fernando Escobar approving the seizure of Mr. Santos' property. After receiving a death threat two days before he was murdered, Felipe Rosenberg decided to record details of the incident just in case he was killed. He accused the president, the vice president, and Mr. Soto in the murder of Mr. Santos, his daughter, and his own."

Thomas and Chavez sighed heavily, breathing in unison as they digested what they'd just learned.

Thomas changed the topic by saying, "There's something else bothering you. What happened? That girl from the protest didn't call you?" he asked.

"She found out that he's a whore. She doesn't want anything to do with him," said Chavez. Jorge wasn't going to let the others think that he didn't succeed in sexual conquest. "You guys know that would never happen. We went out the other night for drinks. We sat in a booth, ordered some appetizers, and started taking shots. She was shy when we met, but after a few shots, she started getting real friendly," said Jorge with a big smile on his face.

"What did she do?" asked Thomas.

"She was rubbing my dick the whole time, jacking me off under the table," admitted Jorge.

"Did the waitress say anything?" asked Thomas in disbelief.

Jorge laughed and said, "No, this girl moved like a ninja." The others laugh hysterically.

"How old is she?" asked Chavez, who was admiring one of Thomas' oil paintings.

"Eighteen, still in high school," confirmed Jorge as his smile changed from a mischievous grin to a clownish laugh.

"Damn Jorge, I'm not surprised. It's always the same shit with you. You meet random girls, take them out on one date, and get laid every time. The sexual stars align for you, my friend," said Thomas.

"Wait, I didn't tell you the best part. Guess who was there?" continued Jorge. Thomas already knew who it was by noting the change in his tone of voice. It was a mixture of disbelief, excitement, and heartbreak.

"Let me guess, Helga." Thomas and Helga were well acquainted. "Your ex hates me, Jorge. It's bad enough that she blames me for the breakup. On top of that, I have to see her every day in class," said Thomas in frustration.

"Didn't she introduce you guys to each other?" asked Chavez. "Yeah, Thomas was going out with Karen, Helga's best friend. They invited us to Karen's house, and we were drinking a couple of beers at the father's bar when I asked Thomas out of nowhere if he liked hippy things," said Jorge. Thomas laughed and added, "There was a weird moment of silence. Then I looked at him and said yes. I didn't know if Jorge was testing me to get dirt or if he was serious about smoking pot." Jorge laughed as well and said, "The piece of shit looked all nervous when I asked him. We ended up taking the girls back to my house to fuck. Thomas was in the bathroom with Karen while I was in the bedroom with Helga," said Jorge.

Thomas interrupted to add, "... halfway in the middle, we switched rooms. Jorge took Helga to the bathroom, and I took Karen to the bed. Then we dropped them off and went back to Jorge's to smoke a joint."

Thomas grabbed a six-pack of beer from the refrigerator while Jorge continued the story. "Anyway, she was there with her new boyfriend. When I noticed her, she was staring at me. I knew she was pissed to see me with another girl," he said.

Thomas handed everyone a cold beer. "Did the boyfriend see you?" he asked in the hope of hearing that there was a confrontation.

"Yeah, he saw me. He put his arm around her like this," Jorge stood up to mock the seriousness on the boyfriend's face.

"He's still scared from the last time. He knows it's not

convenient for him to say something," claimed Jorge. "Yeah, that's why everyone in class hates him," said Thomas about Jorge. "We all went out to drink after an exam, and Helga showed up with the guy. I got drunk and called Jorge to tell him. This idiot shows up all pissed and jumpy. They ended up going outside and having this big argument in front of everyone," Thomas told Chavez. "That's why she hates you, Thomas," replied Chavez. Thomas didn't argue with the comment.

Chavez went to grammar school with Jorge and Helga. He witnessed their young romance and the ugly breakup. "Are you still in love with her, Jorge?" asked Chavez. On the outside, Jorge completely rejected the notion.

"Eat shit. I can't love her. She's crazy."

Chavez and Thomas looked at each other because they knew that wasn't the case.

"We were together for nearly five years. After my parents divorced, she was there for me when I needed someone. Her parents treated me like one of their own kids. And when I left for Europe for nine months, she waited for me the entire time. So, it's not like I can forget about her from one day to the next." It had been nearly two years since they broke up. Jorge wasn't only in love with Helga. He was lost without her.

Six beers and two joints later, there was a knock at the door. All Thomas could see through the peephole was a green baseball cap. "Open up and save me from this woman's madness," said Victor Calderon.

Thomas opened the door and asked, "What the fuck? What's wrong?" Victor walked inside and said joyfully, "Her exams are making her go crazy, and I don't know how much longer I can take living with her."

Victor strolled through the apartment, happy, uninvited, and looking for a good time. He was from a place called Trujillo on the northern coast of Peru.

"What is she crying about this time?" asked Thomas. "I don't know. I moved here to help her out while she earned an MBA. Now the woman thinks she can control my life," complained Victor. He didn't work, go to school, or put any sort of pressure on himself to make something out of life. His journey was all about experiencing people, places and enjoying the moment. Unlike Thomas, Victor didn't seem to put the weight of the world on his shoulders. In a way, Thomas was jealous of that. He wished that for just one minute, he could relax his mind and find such peace.

Victor put a bottle of liquor on the coffee table. "A little something to start the party," he said in a festive tone. "It's called Pisco." Chavez was intrigued by the new liquor.

"You mind if I try some, Victor?" he asked.

"Go for it, man. That's why I brought it."

Chavez uncapped the top and smelled the purity of the alcohol. He looked at the others and said, "Salud." He tipped his head back and drank a shot of warm Pisco.

"So, what are the plans, boys? It's a long weekend. We should enjoy it," said Victor.

"Do you want to try some mushrooms tonight, Victor?" Thomas knew that Victor didn't do any drugs but hoped that, eventually, he would give in to the temptation.

"No, No, I'll leave that to you crazy guys. Tonight I'll just be drinking," he responded. "Well, you might not have a choice. I think we're going to Twisted Mushroom tonight," said Jorge in an attempt to assist Thomas' peer pressure.

Thomas was excited to experience an electronic party in a third-world country, but there was something that plagued him. They didn't have tickets. Jorge somehow had the idea that they were going to the show without tickets.

"How are we going to get in?" he asked Jorge. "C'mon, man! You don't need to ask that shit. Just follow your friend Papi George, and he'll get you in," replied Jorge with confidence. Thomas had no choice but to trust him. Jorge was the type of guy who would find a way to make the promise he made happen.

They got off the couch and headed to the door without having decided where they were going before the show.

"Hey, Thomas," said Chavez. "Why don't you sell me one of your paintings?"

Chavez had always admired Thomas' abstract oil paintings.

"You don't want to buy that. It's not worth anything," said Thomas. He was his worse critic. The time in Guatemala had been very lonely for Thomas. He used that loneliness to rekindle his passion for his art. The more he felt overwhelmed with his life, the more he retreated back to it for clarity.

"What are you trying to say with this?" asked Chavez.

Thomas wasn't comfortable explaining his art. He was the youngest of four male siblings, and soft emotions were something to be suppressed. "It's abstract. It's my portrayal of the journey into the afterlife," replied Thomas. "We'll talk about it when we get back," he told Chavez to get him out of the apartment.

They took the elevator to the garage. Thomas offered to drive because he had recently added new shocks to his Mitsubishi Lancer. The car's engine was overhauled, and he used all his money to pay for a new intake system, turbo system, headers, exhaust, strut bars, rims, and bullet-proof windows.

"Did you fix the bumper you damaged at the quarter mile?" asked Jorge, who often accompanied Thomas to the racetrack.

"Better yet, I fixed it and put on a front bumper guard," said Thomas as he pointed out the latest modification. Thomas loved his car. Mechanics and street racing had become a hobby for Thomas. It was something that he picked up while living in Guatemala.

They all sat in the car, and Thomas asked, "So where are we going?" He looked at Jorge, who was clueless. Jorge looked at Chavez, who was in the back seat.

"Why don't we go to Las Cien Puertas?" Victor said. He often repeated the first word he said when he was excited. The idea was intriguing to the others. Las Cien Puertas was located in Guatemala's historical district, zone one. The location wasn't the safest, but it was a good place to start looking for girls. Thomas turned on the ignition, and the headers roared. He drove out of the underground parking garage and towards the destiny that awaited all of them.

Chapter Two
The Wild West

The drive to Las Cien Puertas was delayed by a murder that occurred on Avenida de las Americas during the afternoon rush hour. Three lanes of traffic merged into one as police tried to move cars, overcrowded buses, and motorcycles around the crime scene. A large crowd had gathered along the curb. They wanted to catch a view of the destruction to ease their curiosity.

The four of them were still eight car lengths away from the bloody massacre. Thomas leaned his head out the window to try and get a better view of the crime scene. People were yelling and screaming in the distance.

"What do you see?" asked Jorge.

"I'm not sure. I just see some police standing around a truck," he replied.

Victor tried to get a better glimpse as well and saw a woman crying while others were trying to hold her from falling. The four of them anxiously waited in the car as they inched closer to the chaos. They all expected to see a dead person, but the sight that followed produced an empty chill of compassion for everyone involved. Two men in their mid-twenties sprinted alongside the car.

"That's my old man! That's my old man!" one of them yelled. They both stopped and looked in horror at their dead father. They fell to their knees and held each other, screaming out their pain to the heavens.

At that point, with the windows all rolled down, Thomas' car passed in front of the gruesome scene. The car looked like it was hit by a bomb. The driver was still behind the wheel, missing most of his head.

"Only an AK-47 can do that," mumbled Thomas while staring at the disfigured corpse. It wasn't the first dead body that he'd seen in Guatemala, but it was the most graphic. "Why don't they cover that shit," said Jorge as they drove by the police. Detectives were investigating blood patterns on the roof and doors in an attempt to recreate the attack. Thomas steered the car slowly into the middle lane. He felt uncomfortable as the woman at the scene bawled at authorities for answers. "Injustice for my son! Injustice for my son!" she yelled.

Everyone in the Lancer remained quiet after passing the gory scene. Jorge and Chavez were angry about what they saw. They'd just encountered another depressing example of their country's instability.

"That's the shit that makes me want to leave this damned place. There isn't a day that goes by where you don't see or hear about a murder. I'm sick of this," said Jorge in disgust.

Victor looked away and pretended the scene wasn't happening. He didn't like downers. Thomas, on the other hand, took a silent moment of reflection to grasp what he had just seen. Over the previous couple of years, Guatemala gradually stripped away any remaining innocence he had with all the violence, poverty, and suffering that he had been exposed to. It wasn't easy for a middle-class American from Boca Raton to adapt to such horrific images. Having been taken away from his sheltered life and then placed in one of the most unpredictable places in the world made Thomas value the privilege of being an American.

"I love this country too much to see it be a warzone for the son of a bitch murderers that run around doing whatever they want," said Jorge. He paused to take a hit from his pipe. "It won't end as long as we have a piece of shit president like Colom."

"If he's such a piece of shit, then why do the people elect him?" asked Thomas.

"Because he wins the vote of the indigenous," said Chavez as he took the pipe and lighter from Jorge's hand. He took a hit and then said, "It's that there are so many people who are uneducated and poor and don't know any better. So, the president promises them a whole bunch of things, like an extra yearly bonus, and they vote for him." Chavez passed the pipe to Thomas.

"That's why we need to revolt," added Jorge with sincerity.

"Be careful with that, Jorge. My dad studied at San Carlos in the early seventies. He was there during the time when rebel forces and University representatives, including him, organized against President Arana after he gave the military power to control the pueblos," said Thomas. The others had never heard of the origins of Thomas' family. They were surprised at his deep roots in the country.

"What did your dad do?" asked Chavez.

"He and a bunch of other students sided with P.G.T and organized protests around the city." Thomas then pointed to his right shin, about four inches under the knee, and continued, "He has scar tissue from a bullet hole right here. He refuses to tell me how he got it." The other three clung to every detail of his words. "He also told me how they protested against selling mineral-rich lands to a Canadian mining group because the government and military had intentions of cashing in on the deal. The government formed death squads who publically executed students and professors; thousands of people died in the genocide."

Thomas may have been an American, but his Guatemalan roots were well-embedded. "And how old is your father?" asked Jorge.

"Sixty," said Thomas.

"My dad is about to turn forty-five. He was in law school at San Carlos when the guerillas took over the Spanish embassy in the eighties," he replied. By that time, natural and political occurrences had changed the course of Guatemala's future.

Disorder spread like a plague after the earthquake of 1976, which left 23,000 people dead and over 1,000,000 people homeless. The majority of those who lost their homes were the indigenous shanty dwellers that lived outside of the capital. They were from pueblos, where education and social structure were non-existent. The earthquake increased their misery to its boiling point.

Thousands of people, with no concept of an ordered society, descended from the mountain ranges to the capital and settled in masses wherever they wanted. The once prosperous and peaceful city would never be the same again. The government had no solution on how to handle the situation they created.

Civil entropy became uncontrollable. For over thirty-five years, the indigenous saturated the city with a selfish attitude, squalling in poverty with little regard for the law. Eventually, as is always the case, poverty yielded crime. Ignored youth created street gangs and affiliated themselves with narcotics dealers to earn money.

They drove down Seventh Avenue, past El Liceo prep school, down to zone one, and made a left onto Seventh Street. Thomas couldn't get the crime scene out of his mind. But, as much as it left an impression, he'd become numb to the violence. It was an everyday occurrence. He came out of his train of thought as they drove by the National Museum.

"That shit is haunted by Ubico's wife," said Jorge.

"Who is Ubico?" asked Thomas.

"An old president of Guatemala," replied Jorge.

The one-way streets and avenues of zone one provided plenty of potholes for Thomas to test the new shocks he installed on the car. He drove much faster than the speed limit.

"Aguas! Aguas!" said Jorge to alert Thomas to be careful. "Make your next left after the parked bus. There's a parking garage there." The blazing car turned into the garage at high speeds, and the exhaust system's maddening roar set off the alarms of all the cars they passed on the way to the third level. Thomas drifted the car around the turn.

"Fuck, Thomas! My balls are in my throat," said Chavez with one hand tightly gripped on the door handle.

"Concha tu madreee!" said Victor as he held on to his Quicksilver hat with both hands.

"You're going to kill us, you piece of shit!" yelled Jorge.

Thomas, Jorge, and Chavez smoked one last bowl of weed in the car before leaving. Victor stepped out. He used the tinted window's reflection to fix the brim of his hat and give himself one final look. The doors opened five minutes later, and the car released a giant cloud of smoke as the others got out. They left the parking lot after paying the guard and walked across the street. Jorge felt alive.

"Tonight, Thomas, anything is possible," he said as he put his arm around his American friend.

In the late nineteenth century, Spanish architecture was complimented in medieval fashion with the dim, yellow streetlights of the night. The buildings didn't look as rundown as they did when the sun was out. There wasn't any traffic and almost no vendors on the streets, making zone one feel safer at night than during the day.

It started to drizzle as they walked towards the central arches that went over Seventh Street. Thomas and Jorge were smoking a cigarette to maintain their buzz until the first round of beer was bought. They walked to the gated entrance of Las Cien Puertas, where there was a crowd of people standing outside. Some were eating steak tacos sold by the lady with the hot food stand. Others were buying cigarettes from a young boy's cigarette and candy stand.

Thomas noticed a homeless woman standing a few meters behind two little girls, probably her daughters, who were asking people for spare change. Thomas studied the way the girls methodically worked their way through the crowd. He always took an interest in the bright tactics that homeless Guatemalan children used to survive. In this case, the girls covered both areas where currency was being exchanged. The taller girl worked the line of people waiting for food while her shorter sibling stood by the cigarette stand.

Jorge found himself alone at the gate. The others were

dispersed among the crowd. He looked around a few seconds before he found Chavez and Victor standing by a Toyota pickup and Thomas by the taco stand, giving the taller homeless girl money.

"Hey!" He whistled, using two fingers to get everyone's attention. They assembled at the gate and passed through, one by one, after being patted down by a security guard while another armed guard stood firm with a shotgun. They were now inside the extended courtyard that was surrounded by one hundred doors. It was two floors with twenty-five doors at the top and twenty-five doors at the bottom of both sides. There were bars that ran along the first floor, some of them with second-floor balconies where people gathered among Guatemala's urban crowd. Each bar had a different style of music playing. This created a mix of gangsters, rockers, tourists, businessmen, rancheros, and potheads all in one place.

Chavez noticed a familiar face in the crowd at the same time the person noticed him. His name was Juan Pablo, and he used to be neighbors with Chavez.

"What the fuck, man? Good to see you," said Juan Pablo to Chavez as they embraced one another.

"I'm over here smoking with my brother and some other people if you want to come," said Juan Pablo. Chavez became eager. He wasn't necessarily fond of large crowds, but he almost never turned down an invitation to smoke for free.

"Your brother's here? I haven't seen him in a long time since he went to the States," said Chavez.

"He's over there. Come on, let's go find him before he finishes all the weed," said Juan Pablo.

"Let's go then," said Chavez before following him to the far end of the courtyard. He nonchalantly sat down along the wall and took his place in the rotation. It was where he felt most comfortable.

Meanwhile, Jorge, Thomas, and Victor followed the sound of a guitar band into a bar that didn't seem as crowded as the others.

"Where the hell is the music coming from? There's hardly anyone here," said Thomas as he admired the Antiguan-style bar with all sorts of rock and hippy memorabilia hanging from high walls. There were Indian masks, pipes, guitars, candles, and artwork.

"Let's go upstairs," said Jorge as he led the way. The creaky, wooden stairs wrapped around a wall and took them to the second-floor bar. The light was dimmed with candles, and raw paintings from local artists hung on the walls. It was crammed with people who sat on their wooden stools around wooden tables, drinking, laughing, and listening to a cover band sing classic rock hits.

Jorge was thirsty and tried grabbing the attention of a waitress. She ignored him because she didn't want to forget the large order of drinks for a table of ten. It was also hard to hear. The noise created a muddled sound wave all throughout. The servers were busy carrying buckets of beer back and forth from the bar to the tables. It was a packed house.

They were about to leave for another bar when Jorge spotted an old friend, Natalie, who was there with her girlfriend, Marissa. The girls had managed to find a table that was located in front of the stage, and, coincidentally, there were three empty stools. Jorge walked over to greet Natalie. She was a former classmate of Jorge and Chavez.

"I haven't seen you since the party at Helga's house. Is she here?" asked Natalie as she looked around to see if Helga was with him. It had been nearly three years since Jorge last saw Natalie.

"No, where have you been? We broke up almost two years ago," he said. Jorge thought the topic was killing the mood. He'd rather drop it. He quickly introduced his friends. "Hey, these are my friends, Thomas and Victor. They're not from here."

Thomas greeted Marissa and took a seat next to her. She fixed her hair before extending out her hand to greet him back. Thomas gently gripped her hand and gave her a soft kiss on the cheek. Marissa shivered and blushed.

Thomas noticed that there weren't any drinks at the table. He used it for an opening line.

"Have you ordered drinks yet?" he asked.

"No, we were about to, just before you guys showed up," said Marissa.

Thomas smiled at her and said, "I'm looking forward to the company." Marissa was charmed by his boldness.

"The feeling is mutual," she replied. They briefly took their eyes off of each other to acknowledge the band, but the attraction was strong, and their eyes locked once more.

Jorge and Natalie were busy getting reacquainted. "So, how are you, Jorge? You look handsome like always," she said.

"Ah, this face gets better by the day," he replied. They both laughed.

"That's what I like to hear," she said.

"I'm working at a bank and studying business at the university."

She was impressed to hear that he was doing so well. Natalie always thought Jorge was attractive, but he was never available.

"And do you have a girlfriend?" she asked bluntly.

"No, I'm not even really looking for one. I'm enjoying the single life," he said.

"Do you still talk to Helga?" she asked.

"No, we don't talk anymore." Jorge pointed at Thomas and said, "He goes to school with her."

Jorge didn't have much else to say about Helga. He would rather talk about anything else. Unfortunately, Natalie insisted on talking about the subject.

"So, what happened? You guys were together since middle school and all of high school." Jorge couldn't escape his past, which made it harder for him to let it go.

Victor was in his own zone, his body reacting to the buzz of the crowd. He wanted to release the harnessed anger. He felt it wasn't good for his aura. He flagged down a waitress and ordered two buckets of beer. He needed the alcohol washing down his throat and into his blood.

Marissa was friendly by nature and was also interested in getting to know Victor. It was obvious to her that both men weren't from Guatemala. She picked up Victor's unusual accent while he ordered the drinks.

"Where are you from?" she asked. "I'm from Trujillo, Peru," he replied.

"Ah, I could tell by your accent that you were South American. What are you doing in Guatemala?" At that moment, Victor had two choices. He could have lied and invented some interesting story in the pursuit of sex, or he could tell the truth and protect what he had with Kayla. Marissa wasn't necessarily his type, so he went with the truth and said, "I moved here with my girlfriend because she is getting an MBA at Francisco Marroquin. Her father is a diplomat in Peru, and he's paying for her apartment. So, she asked me to come." Couples didn't typically live with each other before marriage in Guatemala, so Marissa found the situation a bit inappropriate.

"Does her father know that you're living with her?" Marissa asked.

Victor shrugged. "No, we're lovers on the run," he said.

The waitress returned with two buckets of beer in metal pails that were filled with ice. At the same time, the band graced the stage after a ten-minute break. They tuned their instruments and started the final set of the evening. Each member was dressed in black, the lead guitarist, the bassist, the drummer, and the keyboard player. Marissa could hardly see the band, with Thomas' broad body blocking her view.

"Excuse me; do you think you can move your seat a little more against the wall? I can't see the stage," asked Marissa in an attempt to also regain his attention. Thomas seemed to have lost interest once she started speaking with Victor.

"Yeah, of course," he replied.

"Thank you. I'm sorry. I'm just really short," said Marissa.

"No, don't worry. If you want, I can sit you on my shoulders so that you can have the best view in the house," said Thomas jokingly.

The band was rocking the stage, and everyone in the bar was moving to the rhythm. There were people singing and clapping to the beat, and some even got up to dance. Victor was doing all three, a combined flamenco rendition. He chanted the song's hook with the rest of the crowd.

"Red, Red, Wine..."

Thomas was drumming on the wooden table. He was feeling the vibe when an unknown woman wearing a thin, cotton spaghetti strap tank top sitting across the room caught his attention.

The young woman sat with a burly caballero who appeared to be more than twice her age. Thomas noticed that the girl was being ignored. He stared at her, smiling at her prettiness. It wasn't long before she sensed that she was being admired. The woman was moved by Thomas' classical good looks. She was intrigued by his deep stare, as though he could see into her lonely soul. Her green eyes were seductive. Her body swayed from side to side as she sipped from her bottle of beer. She and Thomas shared wordless communication that was driven by sexual emotion.

Thomas had long forgotten about Marissa as he continued to stare at the girl across the room. The sexual tension was rising. The mysterious beauty took a last sip of her beer, stood up, and walked through the crowd toward the bathroom. Thomas eyeballed her every step of the way until she turned around with a smile and looked at him as if they were the only two people in the bar. He finished his beer and followed her, leaving Victor and Marissa at the table.

The girl was standing in a narrow hallway that led to the restrooms. She was looking at the selection of cigarettes in the cigarette machine. Thomas stood right next to her and pretended to do the same thing. He knew that she was waiting for him to say something.

"I can get a better look at you from in here," he said.

She turned to him with a look of interest and replied, "You're an American, right?"

"How did you know?" he asked.

"You have confidence. Men around here always have a look as though they're still trying to hide in their mother's tits," she said while staring at a pack of Camels.

"What's your name?" he asked.

She turned to him and said, "Tatiana."

"I like it, and it's sexy. Where are you from?" asked Thomas.

The noise pollution was overbearing. They could barely hear each other, so she leaned forward and said in his ear, "Coban." Her lips brushed and tickled his ear lobe, producing good bumps down his neck.

He turned his lips and responded in her ear, "That explains why you're so beautiful." It was his personal opinion that Cobaneras were the prettiest of Guatemalan women.

"Your eyes are so interesting," she said. "They have a story inside."

Thomas was flattered. He gently placed his left hand on her hip.

"I wish we had more time so that I could tell it to you.

"Thomas and Tatiana stared at each other, enjoying the opportunity of being in one another's company. It was a rare moment when two unknown souls acknowledged the same feeling of connection for one another. The numbness in their legs signaled a moment of boundless freedom that they were meant to experience. Then the band started playing their final song of the night, Hotel California by the Eagles.

"Do you want to dance?" he asked.

"I would love to," she replied.

Their hips pressed firmly together as they let the song take over the movement of their bodies. Tatiana whispered the words along with the band, "On a dark desert highway, cool wind in my hair..." Thomas liked that she knew the words to such an amazing song. It told him a lot about her personality.

He whispered back, "Warm smell of colitas, rising up through the air..." Thomas gently nuzzled his lips on the side of her face, towards her ear, making the light peach fuzz on the back of her neck stand. Their bodies swayed from side to side while their cheeks faintly rubbed together. Tatiana closed her eyes and let the energy seep into her body. Thomas held her close, staring into her eyes before sharing a meaningful kiss.

Thomas and Tatiana were two spirits at the peak of a quarter-life crisis, seeking comfort from the loneliness that hid underneath the masks they wore. They met at a moment when both felt lost. The setting became magical once everyone in the cantina joined in singing the chorus.

Jorge had gone out to smoke a cigarette with Leslie. He was surprised to find that his friend had connected with a gorgeous woman. He snuck up and wrapped his arm around Thomas' neck. "Orale, Thomas!" he yelled. Jorge let out a screeching whistle before everyone in the bar joined in to sing the words, "Welcome to the Hotel California!" There was jubilation in the air. Every person in the bar chanted the celebratory song that set the tone for what was going to be a monumental evening.

Thomas and Tatiana held one another close and kissed until the last note was played by the guitarist, marking the end of their moment. Their experience had taken its course, and it was time to say goodbye. There was no exchange of phone numbers or any talk of seeing one another later. Thomas looked at her face one last time and rubbed his thumb on the skin below her eye. She smiled and looked down at the floor to hide her sadness. She wished there was more time to feel loved in the strangers' arms, but that was impossible. Tatiana kissed him on the cheek before turning her head and walking away. Thomas kept his eyes locked on her to see if she would turn around one last time. She didn't. Tatiana disappeared into the crowd, and they both went back to their separate lives.

At the far end of the courtyard, Chavez was smoking a joint with a group of modern-day, Central American hippies. It was often the same crowd that, coincidentally, hung out at the same places almost every weekend. The majority of them grew up in or around San Cristobal. They were all standing in a huddle like Antarctic Penguins in the middle of winter, passing around a long joint that was rolled by Sara, Jorge's cousin from Tampa Bay.

"Damn, Sara, these joints last a long time. I think this is my tenth hit," said Chavez.

"Well, keep smoking. I'm not high enough. Today I took my last exam, and all I want to do is smoke and get drunk," said Sara, who also moved to Guatemala to try and become a dentist. Edgar was there too. He was talking to a younger, emo girl in the corner. He was trying to persuade her with cocaine and LSD to go back to his car. A second joint was added to the rotation by Richard, a pot-dealing guitar instructor who was also the lead vocalist in a local hardcore rock band.

"Hey Sara, I told you this weed would smoke in a joint. It's sticky, but if you grind it up, it smokes really well," said Richard. Both of his eyes were different colors, one green, and one blue. Despite being a mellow guy, Richard looked like a heavy-set psychopath with his long dreadlocks and multiple tattoos on his face and arms.

"I've been smoking joints all day since you sold it to me, Richard. I've got no complaints," replied Sara.

The smoke session was in full effect when Jorge found the group. He was immediately approached by Diego, another childhood friend, who wanted to confirm with Jorge his plans to sneak into the Twisted Mushroom Festival.

"So what time are you coming to my house?" asked Diego while Jorge took a hit.

"Do you really think that we'll get in for free, Diego?" asked Jorge, who still wasn't fully convinced that the plan would work.

"I'm telling you. The field behind my house leads us right to the back, where all the stage crew works. We'll walk around it without anyone noticing and blend into the crowd once we're inside," said Diego while the others listened.

Jorge poked holes in Diego's plan. He didn't feel like going to jail.

"What about the police? Aren't they going to be patrolling for idiots like us?" he asked. Jorge wanted to believe that Diego's plan was foolproof. He wondered if it was worth the hassle.

Victor decided to walk away from the smoke session to get a better idea of the female selection at Las Cien Puertas. He felt more and more willing to cheat on Kayla with every beautiful woman he saw. Victor was hurt by Kayla's lack of faith. He never expected the pressure from her. In a way, he felt duped.

He scoured the crowd in search of the hottest women around, women who could easily make him forget about his girlfriend. The place was getting more crowded by the second, which raised the odds of finding a drunk woman who was willing to have sex. Victor looked by the rock bar and saw some heavy women having a beer-chugging competition. The women in the ranchero bar were a little too ethnic for Victor's taste. He was about to give up and go find the others when he saw the perfect pair standing in front of the reggaeton bar. He assumed they were Colombian because of their tall stature and accentuated curves.

"Any of you ladies know where I can find some Aguardiente?" he asked. It was a trick question to gain their interest; Aguardiente was the national liquor of Colombia.

"No, but when you find some, will you come let us know? We've been trying to find it all night. It's all we drink," said the blonde model. Victor was excited after hearing their response. It confirmed his assumption.

"Is that all you want?" he asked. They both nodded. "Let's go inside and dance for a bit. I'll get it for us," said Victor, like a salesman who was trying to close a deal. The girls were charmed by his confidence and agreed to the proposal. "I'll be right back. I'm going to tell my friends where we'll be," said Victor as he went back through the crowd to find the others.

Thomas was taking a hit of the remaining joint when he felt someone tug on his jacket. It was Jorge.

"Victor found a couple of Columbians," he said as though there wasn't a second to waste.

"Where's he at?" asked Thomas.

"At the reggaeton club," responded Jorge. They located Chavez and advised him about the girls as well. He was in the middle of a conversation with Sara about the best place to find Shucos, Guatemalan hot dogs, in the city.

"I'm telling you. The best ones are in zone four near El Iga," protested Chavez. Sara disagreed and said that the best was in zone ten by Oakland Mall.

"There, the sausage is thick, and they heap it with their own guacamole dressing," she said. The debate of who sold the most delicious Guatemalan hot dogs was often brought up when people were drunk and high; it was the ultimate munchies food.

The others went inside the dark club with the models. Victor grabbed Claudia's hand, the blonde, and Jorge went with Sandra, the brunette. They found a spot on the dance floor and began to move their bodies to the beat of the music. Victor wasn't sure if he would find Aguar- diente at that bar, so he just kept dancing and hoped the gorgeous woman would forget. Thomas and Chavez stood by a table and scoped the crowd. They weren't as interested in dancing as seemingly everyone else in the bar was.

"Want to get a beer?" Thomas asked Chavez, who thankfully accepted.

They walked back through the crowd and asked the bartender for two liters of Gallo. Thomas leaned against the fluorescent bar and chugged some beer, thinking about Tatiana. Her face was stuck in his thoughts, and all he wanted to do was see her one more time. He felt he needed another girl to get his mind off of Tatiana.

"Should we go find some women?" Chavez liked the idea.

"Ahuevos Thomas, what else is there to do?"

They found a high table in the back where some indigenous girls were standing unattended. "Shit, I guess the maids like to party after the long week," said Thomas in Chavez's ear.

Chavez gathered the confidence to offer one of the ladies a drink. She shyly refused. Chavez could sense her interest, so he continued with his courtship. Thomas was amused by Chavez's efforts. After scoping the crowd, he didn't find anyone that compared to Tatiana. He wasn't feeling the environment. The crowd mostly consisted of little thugs who were starting to get rowdy.

"They must be drug dealers," he thought to himself.

It made him uncomfortable to be around such unpredictable people.

Thomas's phone rang. It was Mercedes.

"Hi," she said in her sweetest voice.

"Hey," he responded delightfully.

"Where are you? I can hardly hear you," she asked, hearing the crowd noise and music in the background. Thomas was having trouble hearing her as well. "I guess you won't be coming over," she said to him as he walked out of the bar to hear her better. He found an unoccupied corner near the front entrance of the courtyard.

"Sorry, I couldn't hear you," he said.

"Where are you?" she asked.

Thomas didn't want to tell her that he was drinking. "I'm out with some friends. What are you doing?"

Mercedes was upset at his response and said, "I stayed home because I thought I was going to see you. I'm alone at the house and need someone to talk to. But I guess you're not coming over."

Thomas felt guilty for leaving her alone, especially after knowing about her present state of mind, her depression, and her pain. Guilt was often Mercedes' way of luring Thomas to do whatever she wanted him to do.

"Yeah, I'm sorry," he said. "My friends wanted to party one last weekend since I'm going home for the break next week." Mercedes grew jealous. "You'll spend time with them, but you won't spend your last days with me? Don't you want to be alone with me?" she asked in a final attempt to make him change his mind and go over. As much as he wanted to, Thomas had to refrain for fear of what could happen if they were alone.

"I'll see you soon. Don't get mad," he lowered the tone of his voice to calm her nerves.

"It's okay. I'll talk to you later, right?" she asked him.

"Of course," he said. He understood how fragile her emotions were. At no point did he want her to feel abandoned or alone.

"Send me a message when you get home, just so I know you're safe," she replied.

"I promise," he answered.

"You're not going to forget, right?" she asked.

"I swear to you," he reassured her.

"Okay, goodnight," she said.

"I love you," he replied. They hung up, and Thomas went back inside to be with his friends.

Thomas entered the bar and noticed a commotion at the far end of the dance floor where Chavez was. At first, it was difficult to make out who was who. Once he recognized Victor as the tallest in the bunch, he saw Jorge slap away one of the gangsters' hands, who tried to inappropriately touch Sandra. Then, out of nowhere, fists began to fly. Victor had the unfortunate duty of fending off two of the thugs since he was bigger than anyone there. One of them threw a bottle at him. It missed and shattered when it hit a table. Jorge grabbed the instigator, held on to his shirt, and began throwing rights crosses in succession to his face. Chavez kicked one guy in the testicles before he was hit with a thunderous punch from another gang member. He dropped to the floor and got stomped by a couple of guys while nearby people ran out of the bar in a panic.

Thomas' mind went blank, and he ran against the crowd to help Chavez. He struck the first thug behind the head and followed up with a flurry of punches to the other thug, who was still kicking Chavez. He missed twice before landing a left hook to the smaller man's jaw, knocking the guy out of contact. Thomas pulled Chavez up from the floor and looked to see if Jorge and Victor needed help. They were able to hold off their attackers, but things had reached a boiling point, and someone was going to die if they stayed any longer. Thomas pulled Victor by the shirt, and everyone bolted towards the exit. They ran out of the bar and out the front gate towards the parking garage.

Chapter Three
Just Follow Jorge

There was plenty of time before they had to rendezvous at Diego's house. Thomas drove around the city streets while everyone thought of somewhere to go until then. Jorge couldn't help but notice all the prostitutes lined up along the avenues. Some of them wore short dresses and pumps, while others were less obvious and wore ripped jeans with sneakers.

"That's how we're going to send you off, Thomas," said Jorge, who was calmer after the excitement of the fight.

"How?" asked Thomas.

"With a street hooker," his friend announced.

Chavez laughed. "Yeah, Thomas, you need to get yourself a real Guatemalan, not those rich university girls from La Marroquinn," he said.

Thomas laughed and shook his head. Victor was probably the most excited about the idea.

"How much do you think we can get one for?" he asked.

"Probably about two hundred and fifty Q," replied Jorge.

Victor banged the back of the driver's seat with excitement and said, "Pull over. I want to see what kind of offer they give us."

Thomas pulled over in front of a shopping plaza where two ladies were working their territory.

Victor leaned his head out of the car and greeted the women.

"Oye, Mami, how's the evening going?"

The two women cautiously stood while looking at them.

"Everything is good, Papi. What do you want?" Their guards were up for wild youngsters looking for a freebie.

"I have a question. How much for a good time?" asked Victor. He kept his manners and avoided using profanity in front of the women. Instead, Victor motioned a pumping gesture with his fist to signal what he was looking for.

"Three fifty; that includes oral and anal if you want," she said bluntly. He turned around and looked at Chavez, who was shaking his head in disbelief.

Victor felt he could haggle the streetwalker for a better offer. He stuck his head back out the window and called the girls over again.

"I can get a better price around the corner. What about a group special?" he said as though he was the one calling the shots. One of the women walked closer and looked in the car. Thomas said from the driver's seat, "Why don't you show us a little preview of what we're paying for?" At first, everyone thought that Thomas' request was a big mistake. Victor thought that it interfered with his negotiation. To everyone except Thomas' surprise, the prostitute grabbed her top and pulled out her right breast in front of Jorge's face. The others leaned forward to catch a glimpse of the woman's bare nipple.

"Oh, that's firm," said Thomas as he gave it a little feel. Their curiosity was put to rest, and Victor said, "Let's go." Thomas stepped on the gas, almost taking the woman's head off as a result. She stepped back and cursed at the car as it drove away, blasting the piercing sound of combustion from the exhaust system.

The four drunk guys were stupid and giddy. They giggled in the car like teenage boys who had just seen a naked girl for the first time. Thomas drove to see if he could find another streetwalker. It was their impaired judgment that led them to continue wanting to pester prostitutes on the job.

"I think there are some down by Second Avenue. Turn here," said Jorge as he directed Thomas where to go. "We just have to be careful not to mistake them for the transvestites. They're a lot around here."

Jorge spotted two women standing by a tree that was planted on the sidewalk. "Stop there," he said. Thomas followed his instructions and pulled the car next to both women. They were less welcoming than the last streetwalker. The hookers glared at the four guys as if they foresaw the silliness that was to come; it was written all over their drunk faces.

Victor didn't care that the women were staring at them with disdain. He was hell-bent on finding him and his friends some cheap sex.

"Mami, Mami, how much to please all of us?" he asked as though the prostitutes would be the ones receiving the favor. Both girls looked at each other before the one wearing a red leather jacket stepped forward.

"How many are in the car?"

"Four," replied Victor. She leaned down to take a look at their faces to get an idea of their character.

"How many want it?" she asked again.

"All four of us!" said Victor. She shook her head.

"I can only do two for three hundred each," she said.

The other prostitute, who was still standing next to the tree, asked the prostitute in the red jacket, "What do they want?"

Victor waited as the woman went back to consult with her co-worker. The woman in the red jacket turned around and asked him, "Separate or at the same time?"

Victor made a face at her and said, "Separate, of course. We're not looking for that kind of party."

The longer the women consulted each other, the more Victor became impatient. He wanted to do quick business.

"How about four fifty for the four of us?" he said out loud.

"I'm not here to play games. It's better if you keep driving," said the woman in the red jacket. She was insulted by Victor's ridiculous offer.

"Seriously, four fifty for all of us; four dicks for one hole!" repeated Victor. The woman briefly pondered the offer because the business had been slow. She gave a counteroffer. "Three hundred each, it's the best I can do," said the woman in the red jacket as she looked away, arms folded.

Victor held up four fingers on one hand and one finger on the other hand and repeated, "No. Four dicks for one hole! Four dicks for one hole! How does that sound?"

Thomas and Chavez were finding it hard to keep their composure from laughing.

"You might as well jump in the car and make your money,"

added Jorge to help the deal move a little faster.

She responded by saying, "You're crazy; now move because there are other clients driving around."

Victor tried one last time, "Four dicks for one hole! It's the best offer you'll get tonight, Mami. Make some money. Four dicks for one hole! What do you say?"

Thomas, Jorge, and Chavez were laughing hysterically at Victor's desperation.

She gave him a final offer. "I could probably lower it to two fifty per head, but that's it."

Victor stubbornly shook his head and said, "Four fifty, one hole, four dicks. Now get in the car."

The other prostitute walked forward to defend her friend and said, "I think it's time for you to leave if you know what's good for you." The woman opened her purse and exposed the small pistol that she was carrying. Thomas knew it was time to go. He stepped on the gas pedal and drove away.

"Now, where do we go?" said Thomas to Jorge. Once again, they were without a plan.

"I don't know, but the craziness can't stop," replied Jorge before he turned around to see if the others had a suggestion. "We need women," he added.

The answer to their question was obvious and inevitable. They were all thinking of the same thing when Thomas said, "Let's go to a strip club. What's that one by the airport? Le Club?" Jorge's face lit up with excitement.

"Oh, that's right. I've never taken you to a strip club before," said Jorge.

"What better night than tonight?" said Thomas.

It would be his first time attending a strip club in Guatemala. He didn't know what to expect. He was expecting some type of rundown hole, not like the extravagant strip clubs in the States. Jorge didn't have much insight about the club either; it would be his first time going too, same as Chavez. Strip clubs in Guatemala had a reputation for attracting high-end drug dealers, which didn't appeal as much to the general population.

They stood at the front entrance of Le Club, hoping that a cheap sexual fantasy could be fulfilled within the hour. Three bouncers wearing black suits patted them down one by one in search of guns, knives, or any other weapon. Chavez jittered when one of the bouncers patted too close to his private area. The guards finished their search and allowed the men to pass.

The doors opened, and they were welcomed by a blasting force of bass that was coming from the DJ's sound system. There was a young hostess standing behind a counter with a register.

"It's going to be twenty quetzals each," she said. She took their money and stamped their hands to allow re-entry.

The lights were low, but the stage in the middle of the room was bright with neon pink and green. Thomas was impressed by the similarities to American strip clubs. They took a seat, and within a couple of minutes, three young ladies dressed as sexy angels came to the booth. "Can we sit with you?" the better-looking of the two asked. Thomas and Victor acted like gentlemen and stood up in order to let the ladies slide into the booth. Victor didn't sit back down. Instead, he wanted to take a better look at the dancer that was spreading her legs on the stage. She mesmerized all the men who watched her curvy body sway during the hip-hop music set.

"So, what do we drink?" asked Thomas, who felt alcohol was all that was missing.

"The drinks here are expensive. I'll probably just get a beer," said Jorge. That wasn't what Thomas wanted to hear at the moment. Despite the cost, he ordered a two-hundred-and-fifty quetzal bottle of vodka for himself and his friends to drink. One of the angels took his order while Chavez became better acquainted with the other stripper. He already had his arm around her like he was staking his claim on her for the night.

"Hey, Thomas, you're going to come back, right?" asked Jorge, who had been wondering whether or not this would be their last night partying in Guatemala.

"I don't know, man. It's something I'm really going to have to think about. I fucking love Guatemala, but I don't think I'm supposed to be here right now. I mean, I'm still mourning my grandfather. I got hepatitis last semester and missed two months of school. Then I got Dengue last month and missed an entire week of exams. I'm tired, you know? My grades suck, and I feel burnt out," replied Thomas with sincerity.

"Yeah, but this is what you wanted; an opportunity to become a dentist. You can't give up halfway," said Jorge.

He didn't believe in quitting.

"That's the thing, Jorge. I don't know why I'm becoming a dentist anymore. I mean, it seems that life is telling me one thing, and I have my parents telling me that becoming a dentist is the greatest thing for my future. In a perfect world, I'd be studying dentistry in the States. But things didn't work out that way for me. This path has become so crazy that I think I need to step away and take some time to think about what I want, what's best for me," said Thomas.

"I get it, man. But remember, this was a goal you set a long time ago. You have to see it through. We all go through things in life where giving up seems like the best answer. Life moves on; you have to forget the past, and you have to stay focused," said Jorge, who had wanted to tell Thomas those words since his grandfather died. Thomas, on the other hand, thought that Jorge should take his own advice. He'd seen how impossible it was for Jorge to forget about Helga.

The stripper-angel returned with a bottle of vodka, some ice, glasses, and cranberry juice for the mixer. She poured everyone a stiff drink before Thomas stood up and raised his glass in celebration of the evening.

"Cheers, my friends." They all touched glasses and emptied the contents down their gullets. Chavez wanted to get the girl seated next to him as drunk as possible. He quickly poured her another drink and placed his hand on her thigh to give her a clear message that she was being courted.

Thomas could still smell Tatiana's perfume on his shirt. Her scent made him forget about the fact that there were naked strippers everywhere in sight. After receiving a lecture from Jorge, he wasn't in the mood to party with the strippers. That didn't stop one of them from trying to get cozy with him. She could hear his accent and was intrigued by the notion that he was a foreigner, a foreigner with money.

"Where are you from? Your accent sounds different," asked the stripper as Thomas stared at the ice cubes in his glass.

"I'm from the States, but I was born in Israel," said Thomas. He chose to play a little game with her by saying that he was from an exotic location. It was a lie to help create a romantic aspect to their conversation, something that Thomas felt all women were looking for. The stripper wasn't as dumb as he thought, and she tested the validity of his word.

"Israel, what part?" Thomas had watched enough CNN to know that he could comfortably answer.

"Tel Aviv." He took a sip of his drink.

"Do you want a lap dance?" she asked.

"How much are you charging?" replied Thomas, who was hoping to hear a low price.

"One fifty, but for three hundred, you can do whatever you want." Thomas knew that she was charging him more than the average price. He didn't intend to spend that kind of money, not on a professional hooker. "Why don't you just sit on my lap for a minute, and we'll see where things go," he said while grabbing the stripper's hand and directing her onto his thigh. She didn't seem to mind. It was a good opportunity for her to take a break from the crowd and focus on taking only one person's money.

"Now that we're both comfortable, what's your name?" he asked her. The encounter with Tatiana left Thomas with the utmost confidence to get any woman he wanted, even a stripper.

"Angelita," she said. He knew it wasn't her real name; it was just a stage name.

"What do you want to do to me tonight? Do you want to be my little angel?"

She rolled her eyes at the unoriginal pick-up line. "Pay the three hundred, and you will see." Thomas couldn't believe that he was negotiating a sexual favor after having picked up a world-class beauty like Tatiana. Still, he was horny and hoped that he could accomplish more than a kiss.

Jorge was pensive and a bit uneasy, while Thomas and Chavez enjoyed the company of the strippers. He felt like a hypocrite for having told Thomas to forget the past and move forward. It was something that he was struggling to do. His buzz had kicked in when he decided to get up from the booth and walk outside to smoke another cigarette.

Jorge stood outside the bar and lit a smoke. The club was located two blocks from his father's old office. It made him think of summer vacations, of the days when he would go with his parents to work. Those days were a long way in the past, but Jorge still felt abandoned. His cell phone rang. He pulled it out of his pocket and saw that it was Helga. He rubbed his thumb on the answer button but didn't press it. He didn't feel like getting into an argument with her. He put it back in his pocket and went on a brief stroll around the parking lot to walk off the anxiety.

His phone rang a second time as he finished the cigarette. It was his teenage sister, Ximena. She was at home recovering from alcohol poisoning. The past weekend, she had to get her stomach pumped from drinking too much alcohol at her own birthday party.

"Hey, did you find my watch anywhere in the house? I haven't seen it since the party," she asked with a raspy voice.

"No, are you sure that it wasn't stolen at the hospital? One of the nurses stole my phone when I broke my arm," replied Jorge.

"No, I remember leaving it next to the radio," said Ximena. She sighed. "I don't know why I drank so much, Jorge. My stomach has been sore all week. It aches every time I breathe."

"Just get some rest for school on Monday. You have to catch up on a lot of assignments. I'm taking you to school, right?" he asked, even though he already knew he was.

"Yeah, I'm nervous that everyone is going to treat me weird, especially the teachers," said Ximena. "Don't think like that. Everything is going to be fine. Look, I have to go. I'll see you on Monday," he said. It suddenly occurred to him that he wasn't inside with his friends, who were probably having a great time. Jorge hung up the phone, turned around, and walked back into the strip club.

Meanwhile, Chavez was doing his best to charm one of the strippers. "Come with me to the car; I'll pay twenty quetzals just to talk in the car," he said. For some reason, he thought the creepy line would work.

On the other side of the booth, Thomas had actually managed to keep the other stripper's attention. She sat on his lap, rubbing his penis as he thoroughly massaged her back. "Hey Papi, you're making me feel so good. Why don't you take me to the back room where you can have your way with me," she moaned.

"Just stay here, baby. We'll talk about that later," he said. She became offended at his rejection, and it led her to sit up and get out of the booth. Chavez's girl took notice and got up as well.

Chavez couldn't care less. He poured himself another drink while Thomas made the mistake of going after the girls. He didn't agree with their abrupt exit.

"Hey, hey, where are you going?" he dramatically said while grabbing her hand. The girl turned around and said, "You and your stupid friend think this is a free business, and we're just wasting our time. So, excuse me, we have to go," said the stripper. Thomas thought that he could still persuade the girl to go back with him to the booth. Instead of letting her walk away, he lightly grabbed her arm and turned the girl around before saying, "I just want us to keep getting to know each other. Come back to the booth with me. I know there's a connection between us."

He pulled her close and kissed her on her lips while Chavez looked in shock. The stripper was caught completely off guard. She didn't instantly pull away. For a split second, she kissed him back, forgetting where she was and what she was paid to do. It wasn't long before she remembered once again.

"You son of a bitch; who the hell do you think you are? Don't you ever try to kiss me!" The stripper slapped Thomas across the face, cutting him on the lip with one of her nails. She was irate and had to be held back from attacking Thomas. The bouncers and night managers came running to the scene to see what was wrong.

Victor was sitting next to the stage, stuffing money between another stripper's breasts, when he noticed the commotion surrounding Thomas. He walked over to help defuse the situation, but the stripper wouldn't calm down. She yelled at the bouncers to put a beating on Thomas. They were happy to comply with her orders. The men in black suits approached Thomas, ready to toss him out until the night manager intervened. He wanted to avoid an ugly situation. "Just get you and your friends out of here. We don't want your business."

Jorge walked in as the bouncers were escorting his friends out of the bar.

"Hey, what the fuck?" he said in an aggressive tone. "Leave my friends alone." The men in black suits didn't pay much attention to him, and they pushed Thomas through the doors.

"What happened?" he asked Chavez, who was laughing too hard to give a clear answer.

"The gringo tried kissing one of the strippers, and now they're kicking us out." That was all that Jorge needed to hear. He knew that they had overstayed their welcome.

Blood poured from Thomas' bottom lip. He rubbed his tongue along the gash. Tasting the warm, salty mixture of blood particles. "Karma," he said to himself.

"Where's Victor? He was right behind me," said Chavez, who was sitting inside the car. Everyone looked out the windows, but Victor was nowhere in sight. They stepped out to see where he was. Then they heard some commotion from the other side of the parking lot.

"Don't worry! I'm not touching your piece of shit, Chevy!" slurred a voice in the distance. They walked down the parking lot and found him peeing next to a car with his pants down, screaming at two men. As soon as the men saw that Victor wasn't alone, they swallowed their pride and continued walking to the club.

"Can you believe those assholes; they wanted to look at my dick," claimed Victor to the others as they stood laughing at how ridiculous he looked. Victor didn't mind. He took his time to finish his business before pulling up his pants and walking back to the Lancer.

Thomas drove through Vista Hermosa towards the lavish neighborhoods where much of Guatemala's upper class resided. It was located higher in the mountains, on the road that eventually led to El Salvador. Thomas always enjoyed driving through the area because it had the most North American influence than any other place in the capital. It had modern homes, shopping centers, restaurants, and corporate offices. Also, the view from the road was magnificent, displaying the lights of the entire capital.

"Take a right after the Burger Stop," said Jorge. He directed Thomas down a side street that ran off of the main road.

"Is Diego poor?" asked Thomas. He only asked because even though it was an upper-class section, all he saw were little pueblos.

"No way, these pueblos were just here when this area started to get developed. They didn't want to move, so the city just built around them. Diego's father was a doctor who owned a chain of pharmacies. He was killed in a robbery a couple of years ago," replied Jorge.

"Oh shit, I guess that's why he's always so fucked up when I see him," replied Thomas, who automatically linked Diego's drug use to his father's death.

"That's right. He wasn't always like that. He was a clean kid in high school," informed Jorge.

"This is his neighborhood on the left," he told Thomas as they pulled up to an enormous wall with an immense electronic gate.

Diego walked out of his distinguished home wearing a backward baseball cap and thick glasses for his near-sightedness. He took them inside the house and up the stairs to the balcony of his bedroom. It overlooked a large field where the music fest was being held.

"Hey, what the fuck happened? We were all standing in front of Kashba and then saw Chavez running out with the gringo. You guys ran straight to the car and never came back," said Diego.

"We had to take care of some little gangsters. They were messing with our women," said Jorge.

"You got in a fight over some girls who weren't your girlfriends?" asked Diego.

"Yeah, soon after they were talking shit to them, they started talking shit to us. Then one of them pushed me, and I started swinging," explained Jorge as the others agreed with his account of what happened.

Diego's friend Oscar stepped out of the bedroom and onto the balcony. He wore black skinny jeans and a black hood over his black Anarchy t-shirt.

"What's wrong? Does your head still hurt?" Diego asked Oscar.

"No, but I still feel dizzy," replied Oscar.

"What happened to you?" asked Chavez.

"This imbecile and I got our hands on a vile of liquid acid. The guy who sold it to me said to only take a few drops, which would last about seven hours. We split the entire thing and stayed awake for two days," said Oscar.

"We were so obliterated. We ended up getting lost in a cemetery and spending the rest of the time trying to find our way back here. At one point, some dogs started chasing us, and we had to run into someone else's backyard to get away from them," explained Diego.

"I thought it was el Cadejo, protecting us from getting robbed," added Oscar.

"What the fuck is el Cadejo?" asked Thomas.

"It's the mysterious dog that comes out at night to protect the drunks," answered Jorge.

"It's actually two dogs, one that's good and one that's bad. If you see the white dog with white eyes, then you're being protected from something bad. And if you see the black dog with red eyes, then it's a sign that you're about to die," said Diego, who always had a fascination with Guatemala's folklore.

Diego pointed out the location of the venue. The flashing lights could be clearly seen from his balcony.

"How far is that?" asked Jorge.

"A few kilometers. If the houses weren't there, you could see the entire field that we're going to cross. It's about the size of two futbol fields," he explained.

Thomas remained skeptical about the idea and said, "Yeah, Diego, but there are snakes and holes and all other kinds of shit that's going to make it impossible for us to get through."

The others nodded, agreeing with Thomas' point.

"That's why we're going to walk around the field, along the

fence where we can see where we're stepping," replied Diego. He was positive that his plan would work. "As long as we can avoid the cops, we should be able to walk in without a problem. I've been scoping out the setup all week, and I haven't seen a single person guarding the doors on the side." Despite everyone's doubt, they were forced to trust Diego's plan.

Thomas thought it was a stupid and unnecessary idea. The night had already had enough excitement. He didn't want to push their luck any further. After hearing the words 'as long as' and 'should,' he knew that Diego didn't know what he was doing. There was nothing thrilling about the idea of walking around a giant dark field in Guatemala at 1:00 in the morning, drunk and high. He'd rather pay for his ticket, but no one else had money.

The group stepped quickly through the challenging and almost impassable terrain. "What the fuck am I doing walking around a huge marsh in the mountains of Guatemala? This shit sucks!" complained Thomas to Jorge as they all marched through a desolate field under the blackness of night. Jorge was amused by his friend's discomfort.

"Shit, Thomas, you sound just like a woman, complaining and whining."

"We couldn't just pay like normal people?" he added in frustration.

Diego pointed out a light in the distance, which he believed belonged to police who were scoping the field for drug users. It shone in their direction, waving from one end of the field to the other.

"It's pointing this way. Get down," he said to the others to avoid being seen. Thomas and Jorge took a knee behind a dirt mound. Victor and Chavez hid behind a bush while Diego and Oscar scattered to hide behind an old, broken fence. They continued acting like prison fugitives during that entire walk along the property fence, moving through dips, ditches, and dirt mounds until finally reaching a forest where they were protected by the trees.

Thomas tried to make out a path through the woods. The obscurity of the forest made it a difficult task. The grass was short, and the towering trees waived under the moon's glow, creating a labyrinth of shadows that provided just enough light to see where they were walking. Everyone trailed carefully under the coverage of the forest until Diego led them to an open field that displayed the moon's brilliant fluorescence. "Wait here while we go check on the cops," said Diego before walking ahead with Oscar.

The difference between the contrast and the opaque created a setting where the forest was glowing, making every person appear as a shadowy figure where only their silhouettes were visible. While waiting, Victor checked his phone for new messages from Kayla. There were none. Chavez took a knee to rest his ankle, which was starting to feel a bit sore. Jorge smoked a cigarette, and Thomas looked up at the stars.

Out of the darkness, Diego and Oscar returned to give the word that the coast was clear.

"The entrance is right there. All we have to do is walk straight out to the field and up a small hill without them seeing us." For a second, Thomas believed that Diego's plan was going to work.

"Where are the police?" asked Chavez.

"Standing by their trucks, but don't worry. We should be fine," assured Diego.

They stepped out from under the trees and walked to Diego's next checkpoint. Chavez hobbled a bit. There was an old adobe wall from the early nineteen hundreds in the middle of the field. It provided a good place to hide while Diego scouted the people who were walking around in the distance. Neither he nor Oscar could tell if it was wandering ravers or patrol on duty.

Chavez tried not to focus too much on the fact that his ankle was throbbing. He decided the best thing to do for the pain was to smoke a joint. He walked over to Jorge and said, "Hey, Jorge, pass me the rolling papers."

Jorge was scoping out the dark field with the others when he heard Chavez's request.

"Here they are. How are you going to roll it in the dark?" he asked after taking the papers out of his wallet.

"Because you're going to help me," replied Chavez.

The two worked in tandem to achieve a common purpose. Chavez crushed the weed with his fingers into the creased rolling paper, which Jorge held in his hands. He broke up about half a gram and then pulled out a lighter to dry the joint. They each took a couple of hits before Jorge brought the joint over to Thomas, who hadn't stopped analyzing his current state of being.

"Thanks, man, this shit is crazy," said Thomas, motioning around them.

"What, do you want to go back?" responded Jorge.

"No, not at all; it's just kind of funny to see where my life has brought me." Thomas took a hit and continued. "For years, I just sat at my desk with my face in a book, thinking that I was doing the right thing. Now, I realize that wasn't living. It wasn't until I came here and stepped out of my element that I understood the importance of experiencing the world, acknowledging cultural sensitivity, and having an awareness of social issues abroad. I had no idea how one decision could unlock a series of events that can either lead to catastrophe or something absolutely amazing," said Thomas while looking beyond the stars. Then he looked at Jorge as he returned the joint and said, "The last two years were something that I really needed. Thanks, man."

Jorge was caught off guard by Thomas' moment of sincerity. "From the way you were bitching back there, I thought you were mad about something," he said to Thomas.

"The opposite; I've been absolutely free and completely uninhibited these last two years. That's something many people never get to experience, at least not while living in another country," replied Thomas. The evening had been as random as any other evening that he could ever remember. Thomas was no longer thinking about reasons to be upset. The time had come when he acknowledged the blessing that he was given. Whether he was lonely, depressed, or scared, Thomas knew that the last two years had transformed him from the inside out. He'd gained a better sense of who he was and who he wanted to become.

Diego, Oscar, and Victor continued to monitor the figures moving ahead in the distance. Whoever it was, they decided to walk towards the adobe, which put everyone on high alert.

"Get down! Get down!" said Diego to the others. Thomas finished what was left of the joint, and Chavez hid his weed in his underwear.

"Don't forget your watch," advised Jorge.

"These pieces of shit will try to take that watch if they suspect that we're doing something wrong. They're just as corrupt as the politicians."

The unknown figures whispered to one another when they realized that they weren't alone.

"Shit, someone's hiding behind the wall."

Diego could tell at once that it didn't sound like a police officer. He let out a quick whistle to announce they were friendly.

"Who's there?" one of the voices asked. Oscar returned a second friendly whistle before stepping out from behind the adobe wall.

"Who is that?" asked one of the unknown wanderers.

"It's your mother, Edgar," said Diego as he recognized the soft-spoken voice. It was Edgar, the drug dealer, and his roommate, Freddy.

"You had us shitting in our pants," said Oscar as he wiped dirt off his clothes.

"What are you doing here? We thought you guys were the cops," asked Diego as everyone else stepped out from behind the wall.

"The cops are all the way up there, near the entrance. They're not really paying attention to anyone. We just came here to smoke a little and discuss how we're getting in," said Edgar as he noticed Chavez and Jorge finishing their joint. "What are you guys doing here?" he asked them.

"Trying to sneak into the concert with this idiot," said Jorge after finding out the disappointing truth that their walk through the mud and trees had been for nothing.

"There's no way to sneak in," said Edgar. "There are two entrances with event staff, one in the front and one in the back. The cops are just sitting in their trucks, making sure that no one gets out of line." The update was very disappointing to the others.

They stood outside the rave staring at the ridiculously bright sign which read [Twisted Mushroom Fest]. Jorge, Chavez, and Victor were all thinking of ways to get in for free. The entrance was well-guarded, and there didn't seem to be any other way inside the venue.

"We could just buy some cheap tickets," suggested Thomas.

"We're not all as rich as you, gringo," said Jorge. "Besides, if you're patient, we'll find a way in. If we need to pay our way in, then fine, but I'm not paying full price. If that's the case, then we'll just go somewhere else." The louder the music got, the more they wanted to be in the venue. It was already late, and it probably wouldn't be long before DJ Paul Davila took the stage.

Security was tight at the front entrance. There were a few staff members handling the large line of anxious eventgoers, taking their tickets one after the other while, at the same time, dismissing people who had fake tickets.

"There is no way that we're going to get through this entrance. I'm going to walk around the place to see how things are on the other side," said Thomas to the others. At that moment, Jorge's phone rang. His facial expression changed from that of determination to depression. Thomas had spent enough time with Jorge to know which factor could ruin his mood so suddenly.

"What happened, Jorge?" asked Thomas, who knew it was Helga calling him. Jorge didn't reply. He just stared at the phone screen and slipped away into the dark field to be alone.

"Hello?" he said while feeling a sense of coldness in his chest.

"I haven't heard from you all week. Is everything okay?" she replied like a concerned mother.

"Why did you call?" he asked, regretting answering the call.

"I couldn't sleep. I wanted to know that you're okay," she said.

Jorge struggled to reply. Part of him loved the fact that she was thinking of him. Another part of him wanted to remind her that they were broken up, and he wasn't required to check in with her. Perhaps it was the alcohol and the marijuana in his system, but Jorge wanted to send her a clear message that he knew would rile her emotions.

"I'm good. I'm at Twisted Mushroom," he said in a cold manner.

"I can hear the music from here," she said. "You're with Thomas, right?" Helga blamed Thomas for being a bad influence on Jorge and their relationship. She knew that the two were often running around the streets of Guatemala, up to no good. "I haven't been sleeping well. Sometimes I stay up worrying where you are and who you're with," she confessed. Jorge felt that she was still trying to monitor his every move, which pissed him off more than anything.

"I'm fine, believe me. You should try to sleep and forget about me. Worry about your new boyfriend instead. From what I've seen, the two of you are very happy together," he replied, unable to stop the snide comment from spilling out of his mouth.

"Yes, we are happy. And he doesn't cheat on me like you did. You know something, Jorge? Sometimes I wonder, like an idiot, how many girls you slept with in Europe. It makes me sick to my stomach," she replied. A new fight had officially started between the two.

"We aren't together anymore. You continue to try and make me feel guilty for something that happened almost three years ago," he said.

"You embarrassed me! My mother knew, my father knew, our friends knew. Everyone, except me knew. And when they told me, I would deny it like an imbecile," she said.

"Don't come to me with this shit, Helga! You never call to tell me something nice! It's always the same guilt trip from things that you invent in your head," he answered.

Jorge wanted the conversation to end, but Helga continued to nag him with questions and accusations. They spent the next twenty minutes bickering back and forth, reviving all the negative feelings from the past, and erasing any hope for the future.

Thomas walked around the venue to find a way in. It was secured with a wire fence. He walked to the back entrance, where the line was smaller. For a brief second, Thomas thought that he could sneak past the security guards with a large group of people. Before he had the chance, the last person had his ticket ripped, and the group entered the venue. Thomas decided that his efforts were useless. He continued walking to see if there was anything on the other side.

Thomas had nearly walked the entire perimeter of the venue when Edgar stepped out from behind a parked delivery truck, holding a plastic bag. "What's up, Thomas?" he said. They weren't particularly close friends but familiar with one another through weed transactions. Thomas even gave him a ride to an afternoon class one day. "I'm trying to find a way in. I keep telling Jorge that we should just pay, but I don't think he has enough money," replied Thomas. His eyes couldn't avoid the yellow, polymer supermarket bag in Edgar's hands. He had an instinct that there was something special in that bag, something that could make his night better than it had already been.

Edgar went on to tell Thomas about his failed attempt to sneak in with a fake ticket. "I gave the guy my ticket, and he was going to let me in until another security guard walked over, looked at it for a second, and tore it up before telling me to leave; something about the bar code." Thomas was aware that counterfeit tickets had been distributed all throughout the capital. An acquaintance of his who studied engineering at the University del Valle was the one responsible for creating the fakes, using a scanner and simple editing software.

"How do you think he knew?" he asked.

Edgar pulled out another counterfeit ticket that he found on the floor and said, "The barcode is bad. The fakes have it on the bottom, while the real tickets have the barcode on the side. Other than that, they're practically identical." Thomas looked at the ticket and saw that Edgar was right.

As Edgar explained how the security guard ripped the tickets from his hand, Thomas couldn't help but notice the look on his face. His pupils were heavily dilated. He also had a grin that stretched from cheek to cheek. Thomas sensed that Edgar's mind was wide-awake and on overdrive, that there was more to his inhibition other than weed and alcohol.

His curiosity was put to rest as they both walked back to the front entrance. Edgar reached into the bag and pulled out a handful of fresh mushrooms. He shoved them into his mouth and then smiled at Thomas while chewing.

"What do you have there?" asked Thomas with interest.

"Some mushrooms from my cousin's farm, do you want?" offered Edgar. Thomas had eaten wild mushrooms before, but never in large doses. He knew that one bad overdose could cause things to go terribly wrong.

They were a natural hallucinogen that grew in moist areas prominent with cow dung, like farm fields. The idea of "shrooming" at a rave in the middle of a forest in Guatemala appealed to Thomas very much. He wanted to embrace the chance to create another tale in his young life.

"Sure, I'd appreciate it," he said. Edgar handed over the plastic bag and let Thomas take as many as he wanted. He was surprised by Edgar's generosity. In America, people weren't as hospitable with drugs. One gram of mushrooms normally went for ten dollars.

Thomas handed the bag back to Edgar, who didn't want anymore.

"You can keep it; I'm good," said Edgar. Thomas couldn't believe his ears, so he ate another handful.

Edgar thought it was a bit much.

"Shit, gringo; now you're on the train," he said.

Thomas walked around the side of the venue to observe the police's activity. They clearly weren't keeping an eye out for delinquents or anything of the sort. Some were sleeping in their truck; others were joking around in a group. There was even a handful of police kneeling down while cooking steaks on a grill that was assembled with a grid and some rocks. That was the moment when Thomas vowed never to keep his mouth closed in a situation where he felt he needed to voice his opinion.

Thomas had scoured the entire perimeter of the venue. It wasn't long before he found Jorge standing at the entrance. Chavez and Victor were nowhere to be seen.

"Where are the other two?" asked Thomas.

"I don't know. When I came here, they were gone," said Jorge. Thomas called their phones. No one answered.

"I guess we should wait. If we can't find a way in before they get back, then we'll go someplace else," said Thomas.

They chose a spot next to a Mini Coupe to wait for Victor and Chavez. Jorge saw Thomas eating something out of the plastic bag and asked, "What the fuck is that?"

Thomas pulled out a handful of mushroom caps and showed him.

"Shit, how many have you eaten?" asked Jorge.

"I'm not sure. I just keep eating them one by one, like a bag of chips," said Thomas. Jorge graciously accepted the bag and began to eat away all the mushrooms he could tolerate before handing it back. It was the first time he had tried the drug. He could barely stand the earthly taste of soil, stems, and bark. And the notion that he was eating something that came from feces also didn't appeal to him. However, he swallowed the mushrooms in the hope of feeling an effect that would be worthwhile.

As time went by and the show grew louder, Thomas and Jorge slowly started to feel different.

"How do you feel?" asked Thomas.

"I'm not sure, but I'm getting irritated at all these people walking around so fast," replied Jorge. Thomas laughed.

"That's just the shrooms. Unless you're focusing on something, the rest you see will appear fast and distorted," he said in an attempt to guide Jorge through the experience.

"What do you feel?" asked Jorge.

"All the lights are getting brighter and brighter."

They both looked at each other and giggled hysterically, unable to gain their composure for nearly ten minutes.

Eventually, their abdominal and jaw muscles became tired. The initial peak of the mushroom effect had ended. That was around the time when they heard a voice yell out in the distance.

"Jorge! Thomas!"

They turned around and saw Victor standing behind the fence, on the inside of the venue. He and Chavez managed to sneak into the rave just in time for the main performance. Thomas and Jorge were caught completely by surprise. They couldn't believe what they were seeing.

"How the fuck did you get in?" asked Jorge. "One of the guards sold me four tickets for two hundred quetzals," said Victor.

He handed Jorge and Thomas their tickets through the fence. They were elated at the reality that presented itself. The two strutted through a crowd of impatient ravers without tickets and presented theirs to the guard. He placed a bracelet around their wrist and allowed them to enter the venue. Jorge felt as though he'd just won the lottery.

"Oh shit Flores! I told you we'd get in somehow!" Jorge screamed among the electric crowd with his hands in the air as they walked towards the stage. Thomas thought that the moment was perfect.

Chavez and Victor walked over to greet Thomas and Jorge. The four friends slapped hands in celebration of the night's success. They'd accomplished the objective that was set out before the evening started. It was after 1:00 am, and DJ Paul Davila was taking the stage.

All the walking and waiting had made Thomas thirsty. There were food and drink vendors lining the outskirts of the venue. Thomas saw a few people walking around with squirt bottles, which caught his interest. From the look on the people's faces, he concluded that they were squirting bottles with alcohol.

He approached the booth and asked the sexy, raver bartender, "What type of liquor do you pour in the squirt bottles?"

After taking money from another customer, she turned to him and said, anything you want. We have rum, whiskey, vodka, and tequila."

All options sounded delicious to Thomas, but he couldn't ignore the fact that there was Johnny Walker being sold. It was his favorite whiskey.

"Give me a whiskey and Sprite," he said. He watched with joy as the girl filled nearly half of the 32-ounce bottle with Red Label.

Thomas weaved through the immense crowd, looking for his friends and taking squirts of whiskey. People were in a frantic state as they vied to find a spot where the entire stage could be seen. He knew that his friends, who were all intoxicated and tired, would situate themselves somewhere less suffocating. The first recognizable people he saw were Edgar and Diego, who got in by their own means. They were focused on trying to rip an acid hit in half. Thomas knew that the others couldn't be far from that spot.

The squirt bottle of whiskey was welcomed by the others. Jorge, Chavez, and Victor all drank in celebration of their success. By the time Thomas got the bottle back, there was only a little left. He drank the remaining amount and threw the bottle into the crowd before letting the bass control his movement. The electric vibe coursed through his body as he continued to eat mushrooms out of the yellow plastic bag.

Chavez noticed and asked, "What is that?"

Thomas opened the bag, and Chavez's mouth dropped when he saw all the freshly picked mushrooms. He laughed and then stuck out his tongue, revealing the acid hit that was disintegrating in his mouth.

"Edgar sold me some acid!" he said with dilated eyes. Thomas was a bit envious because Chavez was going to receive a far stronger effect from the acid than he was going to receive from the mushrooms.

The base permeated through every cell in the venue: Boom-

Boom, Boom-Boom, Boom-Boom, and Boom-Boom. There were about three thousand people who were all synchronized with the throbbing beat.

Chavez closed his eyes while the acid coursed through his central nervous system. His shoulders coordinated with his knees in a wave-like movement while his head bobbed up and down to the beat of the music. It was a brief moment for him to ignore everything that wasn't right in his life.

Chapter Four
Thomas and the Forest

Thomas was tripping in the perfect environment. The mushrooms took control of his body, causing him to dance in a trance rhythm. His hands were like that of a composer, conducting along with the beats and the bass. He was surrounded by electrified ravers high on ecstasy, but that didn't break his inner focus that blended with the music. Thomas was in his own world, his own music video. The flashing stars from the stage lights pierced every rod and cone in his retinas. As a result of the drugs, Thomas was able to forget about his running thoughts for over an hour. It was a precious hour of peace.

Somewhere between the fifth and sixth song of the DJ's set, the crowds' energy became overwhelming, and Thomas decided that he'd had enough of the show. He looked around to see if the others were nearby. They were nowhere to be seen. Thomas stumbled his way through the crowd and out of the venue. He wandered into the forest, conscious of his actions and hoping to find something that was missing in his life.

Thomas looked up into the night sky, awed at the brilliant array of stars that appeared before him. There were millions of them shining like fine-cut diamonds. The midnight blue sky domed over the earth while the pale moon created a mystical glow over everything the light touched.

He walked over the raw terrain without fear of danger. The tranquility allowed him to listen clearly to his thoughts. Thomas never imagined that his pursuit of being a dentist would one day take him so far away from home. Deep down in his soul, he knew that it wasn't the right time for him to reach that goal. He wanted to believe that there was a greater force guiding him toward his final decision, but at the end of it all, his faith was fragile.

The shadows started taking ghostly forms as sweat drizzled from his forehead down to his neck. He wasn't scared, not like most would be. The grass was low, and he was able to step lightly into the unforgiving abyss. He stood under an opening in the trees that aligned perfectly with the moon. He looked up and thought about his future.

Despite the cool mountain climate, sweat misted Thomas' forehead. He was starting to get nervous that he'd gotten himself lost until he saw an opening through the forest. He didn't know where it led, but it was the only place to go. The forest had become less dense with trees. The moon lit the ground, which helped to guide Thomas out of the dark.

He basked in the magnificent sky that glowed purple. It was alive with energy, much like the sci-fi images on television of a faraway dimension. A gust of wind suddenly brushed against his face, causing him to take a step back, further away from the mountain's edge. The thought of something happening to him while he was alone made him think of his parents and the anguish it would bring them.

"I have to honor them," he said.

Thomas couldn't figure out how to tell his parents that he was stepping away from dental school. He was their golden child who grew into a responsible young man. They were enormously proud that he'd found a different way to pursue dentistry when he couldn't make it in the States. Telling them that he was leaving dental school for good was something that he would have to do alone. There wouldn't be any support or understanding from the people he loved. It was the first step to creating his own independence.

The sky waived from side to side. The hypnotic pattern led his body to freeze for a minute until he realized how fucked up he was. He giggled and then rubbed his hands over his eyes, trying to snap back into reality. Thomas was tripping hard, and there was nothing that could be done about it. As Edgar said, he was "on the train."

He roamed the mountain edge at a turtle's pace, giggling uncontrollably the entire time at the sound of his own breath. The muscles along his back started to tense up more and more the longer he laughed. His jaw muscles were beginning to get sore as the yawning became uncontrollable. Still, he was feeling more alive than he'd felt in a long time. He felt as though he'd been brought to that place for a purpose, for clarity, as if someone or something wanted him to listen to his own thoughts. His phone vibrated. Thomas saw that he had a text message from Mercedes. Suddenly, he stopped laughing. He had yet to take the time to digest everything that had happened between him and young Mercedes over the last two years. Thomas loved her more than anyone else in the world. It was one of the few things he knew was certain. He was convinced that they were two souls destined to be bound forever. Up until the moment they kissed, Thomas had never imagined a love affair with her.

Thomas sat down in the grass. He thought of their childhood to see if there were any signs along the way that their relationship was destined to become so complex. When she was a little girl, practically a baby, Mercedes was very selective about the people she would get close to. But he always had her attention. She was irresistibly adorable with her big brown eyes, fair skin, and curly, chocolate-brown locks. He didn't have a problem carrying her when she needed to be carried or holding her hand whenever she wanted it held. As the years went by, every reunion would follow the same script, she would find him, and he would find her.

Life took its usual course, and they grew up separate from one another in different countries; Thomas into a man, and Mercedes into a young woman. Yet, despite the distance, long periods without seeing each other, and their age difference, the connection didn't fade. With every reunion, a different physical version of the person they last saw would appear. It didn't take long for them to look into each other's eyes and find that person who provided so much comfort. Nothing could alter something so organically beautiful.

Soon after the decision was made that he would go live in Guatemala, Thomas nestled in the thought that he would finally get an opportunity to be a part of her life. It was an opportunity that he'd always welcomed. Mercedes, on the other hand, heard the same news and built an unnerving sense of anxiousness, not believing it was true, up until the day she saw that he'd finally arrived.

Thomas moved in with her family for two months while his apartment was finished being constructed. There, he lived with Angela and Gabriel Ibanez, largely successful freight forwarders and best friends to Thomas' parents. They had two children, Miguel Angel, the youngest, and Mercedes.

The family lived in a two-story home with four bedrooms. The second floor was designed so that each bedroom was its own wing of the house. With the parents at work all day and Miguel staying after school for sports or some other extracurricular activity,

Thomas and Mercedes were often left alone for most of the afternoon. The housemaid was always there, but she usually remained in the kitchen doing her work for the day. And so, through circumstance and coincidence, they were given a special window of time to be together.

It didn't take long for Thomas and Mercedes to become inseparable, like best friends who had years of catching up to do. He would come home from the university at the same time she would come home from school, and they would spend their afternoons talking about their day, exploring his confused adult life or her self-doubting teen years. For the first few months that he was in Guatemala, before meeting Jorge, Thomas would spend his weekends with her watching movies in her room until the early hours of the morning. At the time, it seemed like they were simply enjoying each other's company and nothing more. But unknown to Thomas, Mercedes was slowly falling in love with him.

It happened on a Wednesday afternoon in June. A powerful storm had settled over Guatemala for two days straight, and the slippery mountain roads made it dangerous for anyone to drive. Classes were canceled that Monday throughout the capital, and Thomas decided to spend the rainy day with his younger, beautiful friend. As usual, they were completely alone. Mercedes picked out her favorite movie, a romantic comedy, to pass the time. Thomas wasn't particularly excited about her selection, but she usually got her way with him.

Mercedes' thought process toward Thomas wasn't the same. She couldn't explain it, but Thomas was all that she thought about, and for someone so young, those feelings came with high levels of intensity and confusion. As far as she knew, she was undeniably in love with him.

The movie was halfway complete, and Mercedes could not stop thinking about him. She was nervous because she felt that her urges would be too hard to contain. Thomas hadn't a clue.

Mercedes couldn't think of her opening line to get him to notice her the way that she wanted. Instead, she slowly started making advances with her body. She got close to him and said,

"I'm cold."

"Go and get yourself a blanket from your room," replied Thomas. As he returned his focus to the movie, he felt her head lying on his shoulder. Thomas ignored the obvious until she started to tenderly rub her fingers up his arm. Thomas tried as hard as he could to not make the situation awkward. He didn't want to think that she was hitting on him, but her actions were making that impossible.

Mercedes' breathing became heavier as she pushed her firm breast against his arm. Thomas was starting to get aroused. Mercedes' boldness was unlocking his feelings as well as her own. The situation was at the point where he should have said something to stop her advances, but he didn't. Thomas had a choice and decided to let her seduction continue. He was in a conscious moment where his body and mind were struggling to comprehend the situation at hand.

A warm shock traveled in his blood as her hand moved from his arm to his belt line. Eventually, she pushed enough of her weight on Thomas that it caused him to lay back even more. Mercedes took it as a sign to become more aggressive. Thomas didn't unlock his eyes from the television as she began to rub the inside of her thigh against his leg. His breathing became heavier while his frozen body endured her passionate seduction.

The attractive force between the two was immense. Thomas couldn't stop himself from liking what was happening. He placed his hand on the inside of her thigh and slowly started to rub upward. The closer his hand moved up, the harder she rubbed along his belt line, just above his pubic bone.

Their heads moved closer together. It wasn't long before she was rubbing her lips on his cheek. Thomas had lost all control of the situation. Her lips crept closer and closer to his as his fingertips rubbed her clitoris through the cotton pajama pants she wore. Mercedes pecked the side of his mouth once as if to test the waters. Thomas didn't react. She attempted it again and kissed him in the same place. Thomas kissed back with the side of his mouth. He looked into her eyes and pulled her on top of his chest, with her legs straddling his waistline.

Mercedes rubbed her breasts against his body. Thomas moved his hands close to them but hesitated to caress her. He wanted to, but his subconscious wouldn't allow it. Therefore, Mercedes made a move for him. She grabbed his right hand and placed it under her shirt. Thomas then grasped her left breast and felt instant pleasure.

He kissed her along her soft white neck and up toward her ear as she reached down under his pants and grabbed his erection. She thrust her hips and pumped her right hand three times: up, down, up, down, up, down. Thomas couldn't refrain his pelvis from thrusting back, pressing his penis harder against her pulsing genitals. Mercedes' breathing continued to become heavier and heavier the hotter she became.

Thomas took off her shirt and pulled her close to feel her warm skin against his. While still kissing, he unsnapped her bra, allowing her succulent breasts to fall.

Thomas then picked her up with her legs wrapped around him. He laid her down on the bed and took a moment to admire the beautiful specimen that was her body. He proceeded to kiss her body from the neck down, giving her a strong sensation of goosebumps.

He kissed her all the way down to her belly button and pulled down her pajama pants, exposing her wet silk panties. He kissed all around her pelvis region and thighs until the temptation became too much to bare. Thomas pulled off her underwear and started to perform oral sex. Her body quivered from the unfamiliar sensation, building the pressure until she climaxed.

Since that day, Thomas didn't know how to handle the relationship. He was torn between the guilt of hiding something from both families and the guilt of damaging her psychologically. Mercedes, on the other hand, didn't let her conscious torment her. She was in love with Thomas, and his embrace meant the world to her. It was unexplainable, but she was only happy whenever he was around.

Thomas continued walking further away from the electronic music festival without caring whether or not he was lost. The drugs were causing the synapsis between his cerebral neurons to fire at an unprecedented rate. He couldn't control the random thoughts that were teleporting in and out of his consciousness. One minute he was thinking about family, about how much he loved and missed them, how he wanted to make them proud. The next minute he was lingering on concepts for future paintings. "I need more fire, people without faces; I need to let go, be free."

Then he thought about death and dying. He'd been thinking a lot about death ever since his grandfather passed away. The whole event made him face his own mortality in a way that he'd never had to do. As a philosophy student, the calming peace of la Muerte had always appealed to him. The fear of death was always something that Thomas wanted to conquer. Guatemala was the perfect place for him to erase any fear that remained. For the last two years, he'd been exposed to raw images of horror on a daily basis. He'd never seen a dead body before going to Guatemala. Since arriving there, Thomas had numerous encounters with lifeless corpses left to rot on the streets like a dog.

The gruesome images from earlier in the day were still etched deeply into his mind. Such incidents left Thomas wondering whether or not his life was in danger by staying there. The crimes in Guatemala were getting worse by the day, caused by the growing poverty rate and the abundance of narcotics activity. He was becoming paranoid, feeling that the odds of something bad happening to him were growing with each day that he was there.

Thomas' feet brought him to a cliff. There was nowhere left to walk. He was at the edge of the mountain looking over an enormous valley with the moon above, glowing freely in a cloudless sky. Thomas' eyes lingered on every detail and every color that comprised the heavens. A firefly flew across his line of vision, coming out of nowhere before disappearing into the forest behind him. Then another followed, but it wasn't alone. It was accompanied by a few more glowing fireflies. They flew into the darkness of the trees as well. Thomas looked around and noticed that he was suddenly surrounded by fireflies. The glowing bugs were all present at the same location, around a tree at the forest's edge. Thomas strongly felt that God was using the power of nature to communicate with him. It was a gift, a message that he was still being guided with light by his side.

Thomas eventually walked his way back from the forest and to the venue, where he saw his friends standing at the front entrance.

"How long have you guys been out here?" he asked the others, who were surprised to finally see him.

"The lost disciple appears," said Victor.

"Where were you," asked Jorge. Thomas looked at the time on his phone and noticed that he'd been gone for well over an hour. His body still felt wobbly, and his vision was still impaired. Thomas couldn't stop yawning, and all he wanted was a bed.

"I just went for a walk," he quickly answered. Thomas wanted to keep the experience to himself. "Now, where do we go?" he asked, looking at Jorge. Thomas knew that he had something else planned for them.

Jorge wanted to use the time to do something that he'd always wanted to do with Thomas. He felt that the only way to give his American friend a true Guatemalan adventure would be by taking him to his favorite place in all of Guatemala, *Lake Atitlan.*

"To the lake; let's go to the lake," he said as though a voice in his head was telling him to go that way.

"It'll only take a couple of hours to get there. You just have to be careful with the drive," he warned Thomas. "There aren't any streetlights in the mountains. You're going to have to drive the entire way in the dark," said Jorge. Thomas didn't argue or debate the plan. They were all ready to see where the night would lead. Going home was not an option. "The roads wind the entire way, and if you're not careful, you could drive off and kill us all," explained Jorge.

"I'll get us there, but you guys can't fall asleep. Someone is going to have to stay up to keep me awake." Thomas welcomed the challenge even though mixed emotions coursed through his head. "My dad drove off a mountain when he was a kid, and two of his friends died. One of them was decapitated. My dad was in a coma for almost two weeks. I don't want the same shit happening to us," said Thomas.

"Okay. Let's just pass by a gas station to pick up some munchies and beer," said Jorge.

Chapter Five
The Drive to Atitlan

The Lancer drove west, underneath the darkness of night, toward Sololá, the department that surrounded Lake Atitlan. The drive was dangerous and unpredictable. There were no lights and hardly any inhabitants along the way. Thomas could barely see where he was going.

They drove on a split one-way lane with no median in between. The slightest error or loss of concentration could cause him to crash and get them killed. Outside of where the light touched, everything else was a shadow. The road would curve left and curve right along the mountains' edge. The danger created nervous tension inside the car. Everyone, even Chavez, who was still tripping on acid, lent their own eyes to help Thomas.

"You see, it's not that hard," said Jorge.

"It's like the time we drove to Antigua in the middle of the night to meet that Canadian girl and her friends. The only difference is that this is going to be a longer drive," said Thomas. "But don't worry, it's not a problem," he assured Jorge.

The evening had been waiting for all of them since the day they were born. They were experiencing something precious that no other soul was experiencing. At that moment, Thomas knew this trip was meant to be different. He was ready to drive through any obstacle that stood in the way of their freedom. His time in the forest led him to start believing that the evening had a special purpose. Thomas drove fearlessly through the untamed roads toward the moment of enlightenment that God had chosen for them to experience together.

Everyone else in the car had fallen into their own thoughts. For nearly a half hour, the exhaust system was the only sound that could be heard. Jorge didn't like the prolonged silence; it made him uneasy. He withstood it for as long as he could before taking out his weed case and rolling a joint. Thomas and Chavez noticed. "Just what I need to stay awake!" said Jorge as he licked the joint to allow the papers to stick.

He took his first hit and held the smoke in his lungs. "Puta Thomas!" he said while expertly holding in the smoke. "Here, you're going to see the real beauty of Guatemala." Jorge expelled the smoke from his lungs and continued his awe of Lake Atitlan. "It's an enormous body of water in the Guatemalan highlands that's surrounded by three volcanoes." Thomas listened, but his eyes never left the road.

"This shit that we're talking about is the deepest lake in Guatemala. What I think we should do is get some breakfast, take a boat over to San Pedro, have a smoke, relax by the lake, grab a little lunch, and ride back." Thomas gave a big smile. It sounded like the perfect day to him, especially the part about going to San Pedro. San Pedro was most famous among the stoner crowd in Guatemala. It was a small town located along the lake that was known for being a pothead refuge, like Amsterdam, where people could smoke weed freely on the streets and in the cafes. It was a sanctuary for modern-day hippies.

Jorge continued talking to keep Thomas alert. They passed the joint back and forth while Chavez waited patiently for a hit. It wasn't an easy task because he was still tripping. He needed weed to balance the uneasiness that was occurring in his mind. His nervous system was still on overdrive, his brain switching from thought to thought under the blackness of night. The single light coming from the car radio was enough to create a light-show of distorted images.

The joint brought life back into the car. Thomas felt revitalized from the sleepy effect of the mushrooms. "I needed this shit. Good job, Palma," he said while remaining focused on the road. Jorge was a good co-pilot, making sure Thomas got as many hits as he wanted, playing loud, upbeat music and keeping up a constant stream of conversation to keep the driver awake. Thomas just hoped that Jorge wouldn't get too distracted and miss pointing out the exit to Sololá.

"How do you know where the exit is? I can't see shit," he asked Jorge.

"Man," responded Jorge with surprise. "When do you ever have to worry about anything when you're with me? Don't I always show the gringo a good time?"

Thomas grinned and nodded.

"Yeah, you do, Jorgy boy."

The car was engulfed with smoke, and Chavez had yet to take a hit. He could no longer sit back with his mouth shut while the joint burned away. Thomas and Jorge had each already taken a few hits.

"Shit, guys, are you planning on passing that joint any time soon?" asked Chavez.

"Oh, sorry, man, here you go. Make sure you give some to Victor; he's too quiet," said Jorge as he passed the joint to the back.

"Yeah, usually we can't shut you up, but you've hardly said a word since we left Diego's house," added Thomas.

"I'm just making sure that you don't drive us off a cliff," responded Victor in a dreary tone while busy reading the text messages that he and Kayla had sent to each other earlier that day.

After taking a couple of hits, Chavez's world stopped shaking. He leaned back, closed his eyes, and let the dazed feeling take over his senses. He felt a second rush of euphoria course through his body. The THC from the weed had reacted with the remaining LSD. The acid trip was in full effect once again.

Chavez couldn't control what was happening to him. He turned his head towards Victor and saw his profile change into an image of a dragon. Victor's eyes disappeared, leaving two gaping black holes in their absence. All the while, sober Victor was wondering why Chavez was staring at him.

"Oh shit, this guy flew to the moon, and he doesn't even know it," said Victor to inform the others.

An uncontrollable laugh took over Chavez's body. He tried as hard as he could to compose himself, but it was pointless to do so. The other guys stared at him in varying shades of confusion and mirth.

"Hey Chavez, what the fuck is happening to you?" asked Jorge.

"I don't know. I don't know. I don't know," was all he could say. He curled himself against the car door in an attempt to hide away from the world.

"The joint, pass it to Victor," said Jorge as he noticed that only a roach was left.

Chavez extended his arm to Victor and said, "You've been looking at that damn phone for too long; smoke this instead." Victor hadn't smoked weed in over ten years. He didn't like its mellowing effect, especially if there were girls around. But for some reason, on that night, he was inclined to reach out and grab the joint from Chavez.

"Are you actually going to smoke, Victor?" asked Jorge. They all knew his aversion to weed. Thomas wanted to pull the car over to witness the moment with his own eyes. Fortunately, the road straightened out, and he was able to see through the rearview mirror.

Victor grabbed the joint and looked at it for a second before putting his phone in his pocket. With six eyeballs staring at him, he put it to his mouth and smoked. He held the smoke in his lungs, looked at his friends, and blew it in their faces.

They'd been driving for almost an hour. Chavez's brain had been shut down while Victor sat quietly in the back, drifting away in his own personal meditation. He took out his cell phone from his pocket and again read the three text messages that Kayla sent earlier. The first message said, [Why do you get mad? I only want what's best for both of us.] Thomas noticed through the rearview mirror that he'd been staring at his phone all night.

"How's it going, Victor? Why so quiet?" he asked.

"This girl has me going crazy. She can never shut up about something once it's stuck in her head," he said in frustration. "It's just that we got into an argument before I showed up at your apartment. She doesn't stop bothering me about school and work and what I'm doing with my life. I told her that she wasn't my mother and that she needed to stop trying to dictate my life. I feel like she brings me down when I'm already down, and that's not what a girlfriend is supposed to do," replied Victor.

Thomas let Victor talk. He needed to get it out of his system. "It sounds like she is trying to push you, trying to motivate you," said Thomas.

Victor knew this. His male pride didn't want to allow her to force him to do something. She was the earner in the household, and Victor didn't want her to think that just because she made more money, she could tell him what to do.

"No matter what, I'm always going to do things my way. That's just the type of person that I am. I prefer to take life day-by-day and at a slower pace than most. She wants me to go back to the marketing job I had in Peru, but I told her that there isn't a lot of work for illegal immigrants in this country. I told her that once we get to Peru, I want to find a job with a surf company, something in promotions or public relations," said Victor.

Jorge, still awake, though quiet for most of this exchange, finally spoke up. He was also a firm believer in avoiding unwanted pressures.

"You're right, Victor. Don't let anybody push you to do something that you don't want to do. If she doesn't understand you, then you two shouldn't be together."

Victor was at a point in his life where he wasn't scared to be alone as long as it meant that he could keep his freedom. He neglected to take into account the fact that Kayla was at an age where she was starting to think more about marriage, having a family, and children. Even though he was nearly five years older than her, he wasn't sure if he wanted those things.

He looked at his phone and read the second text message: [Call me when you can so I know you're okay.] Every time that he was reminded about her love, it made him remember all the things he wished he could do for her. At the moment, she was his provider. Victor was a conformist who wanted to change and had all of the abilities to do it, but he didn't know how to focus on a goal. To him, life was simple. He believed that rash decisions shouldn't be made until all the intangibles were in their right place.

The third text message: [I love you.] It wasn't the first time she'd said it, but he didn't know if she meant it or not. It wasn't easy for a man like Victor to comprehend a word like 'Love.' His mind couldn't create an emotion whenever he heard that word. Sometimes, he thought that there was something wrong with him. Girls had been telling him about love for as long as he could remember, but it didn't move him the way it moved other people. It was something too emotional for him to process.

It was after 4:45 am, and the night was about to enter its twilight. Victor and Chavez had fallen asleep. Jorge was still awake, using the time to explore his own thoughts. The mood was peaceful, a good opportunity for honest, heterosexual, male conversation.

"What do you think of Guatemala?" Jorge asked Thomas.

"What?" Thomas was caught off guard. "What do you think of Guatemala?"

Thomas yawned and then rubbed his left hand against his eyes to pull himself out of his stupor.

"I love this place. Once, I came here when I was fourteen and got food poisoning so bad that shit was coming out of my mouth and ass at the same time. After that, I didn't care too much for Guatemala. But now, it's totally different. Guatemala taught me about life. It opened my eyes to so much," replied Thomas.

Jorge agreed and said, "Ahuevos, you've seen a side of Guate that very few Americans will ever know. Not even the rich snobs from your University have experienced this country the way you have."

Jorge was never a fan of the elite superclass of Guatemala's society. That included Thomas' classmates.

"That's true, but the people from my school don't do the crazy shit I do because they aren't stupid. Danger exists in every corner of this country, and they'd rather avoid it. There's crime everywhere you look," said Thomas.

"Yeah, a lot of shit has been going on lately. The son-of- a-bitch president and his predecessors are all to blame. Their greed has driven this country to shit," said Jorge.

"They keep stealing instead of giving the money back to the natives," added Thomas.

"Exactly, they'd rather see millions of people suffer in- stead of giving up their stolen fortunes," answered Jorge.

"The problem is everywhere." Thomas was talking about the poverty, death, and hunger that were abundantly present throughout the city and within the rural areas.

"Yeah, man, there are too many people who were never given the chance to live a normal life. They were born poor and will die poor. You know, sometimes, when I see that, it makes me doubt the existence of God," said Jorge as he looked out the window at the twinkling night sky.

"What do you mean?" asked Thomas.

"How can there be a God who is good when so many innocent people are suffering." Thomas knew the argument all too well.

"It's the problem of evil," he said.

"What does that mean?" asked Jorge as the words attracted his interest. "The problem of evil questions the existence of God in a world where there is suffering. It's an existential question: if there is a God, then why does he let people suffer?"

Jorge was blown away. "You think too much, but I hear what you're saying."

"I know. I have that problem. I always let my mind drift away from these far-off thoughts. I wish I could turn it off," said Thomas. They both sat in silence for half a minute to let Thomas' words sink into their brains.

"But it's a good thing. I never heard anyone talk like that until you came along. You're a shit talker," said Jorge. He meant it as a compliment.

The car approached a section of the road that was being reconstructed because of the mudslide collapse that occurred two weeks earlier. Gravel and dust filled the air as the Lancer moved swiftly through the slippery obstacle. It made it more difficult for Thomas to see ahead. He turned on the high beams and used the mountain wall to his left as a guide to see where he was going. Nervous sweat formed above his upper lip as he navigated the twisting roads.

Thomas maneuvered the vehicle around the narrow curves that

weaved to the left and to the right.

"This is crazy. I can't see shit, Jorge," said Thomas.

"We still have an hour to go. Stay calm," said Jorge, looking at the clock on the car's dash.

"How do you know?" asked Thomas to make sure Jorge was cheerful about where they were.

"Just trust me, man," said Jorge.

"I just don't want to sleep in a place where I can be robbed, raped, and killed."

Jorge laughed as he recalled the evening when they ran out of gas in the mountains in the middle of the night during one of their drunken adventures.

"You stayed up all night, shitting your pants, thinking that something was going to happen," he commented to Thomas.

"Because you had me in the middle of nowhere, and I heard at least three or four gunshots while you were sleeping," said Thomas. The significance of that evening was that Thomas learned an essential lesson about fear. It was created in mind.

It seemed as though they were going to arrive in Sololá without any significant incidents occurring along the way. That was until Jorge saw something unusual in the distance over the jagged horizon. There was an apparition floating in the middle of the sky. The object was un-earthly, unfamiliar to them or anyone else who could see it.

"Shit, man, do you see that?" asked Jorge. He was stunned by the mystical sight.

"What the fuck is that?" asked Thomas as he stared at the glowing fireball that was invigorated with energy and life. Thomas slowed the car down so that they could get a better look at the mysterious figure.

Victor and Chavez were sleeping when they felt the car decelerate sharply. Victor jerked out of his slumber and asked, voice groggy, "Did we arrive?"

No one answered. Thomas and Jorge were busy trying to make sense of what they were seeing. Victor looked to the right and saw the most fantastic thing that he'd ever seen in his life.

The giant burning fireball hovered high in the air. It was orange with a yellow glow, and it flew in the sky without wings or any apparent pilot. The figure was slowly moving away from them in a linear motion. Still, there was more than enough time to observe every celestial detail of its form.

The object radiated with energy. Everyone in the car watched the UFO with their eyes glued and mouths open.

"But seriously, guys, what is that shit?" asked Jorge in a panic as he turned off the radio. Thomas pulled off to the side of the road so they could get a better look.

"I don't know, but let's go see it closer," he replied be- fore turning on his emergency lights.

"You're going to get out?" asked Jorge in disbelief.

"Hell yeah; we all are." He grabbed his cell phone, a cigarette, and a black lighter and stepped out of the car. Everyone else soon followed.

It wasn't easy for any of them to determine the exact size of the

UFO, but it was big. Thomas touched the tip of his thumb with his index finger to form an oval. He pinched the adjoining digits with slight pressure and held his hand up to the sky. It formed the shape of a teardrop, and the UFO's outline fit perfectly inside of it from where he was standing. No one could believe or make sense of what they were seeing.

Chavez had to remind himself that he was seeing something real and not an illusion from the acid.

"You guys are all seeing the same thing, right?" he asked.

Victor broke his silence by saying, "But seriously, guys, what is that?"

Chavez could only respond by trying to reaffirm his sanity. "I don't know. We're all seeing this, right?"

Victor took the phone out of his pocket to get proof of what they were seeing. Everyone else followed his lead. The figure gradually began to float away while they filmed and took pictures. They all stood speechless while staring at the craft that grew smaller and smaller. It was as real as anything that they'd ever experienced, but no one could fully accept what was happening.

The UFO eventually disappeared behind a far-off mountain ridge. The four friends let the silence of the night gradually soothe away the shock. No one had an explanation. They just stood there and looked around to see if anything else would happen; nothing else did. The moment was over. God had spoken, and whether or not they were aware, they all listened.

Jorge opened his mouth and said, "Welcome to the Jungle, you fucking aliens!"

It broke the tension. The others exhaled their breath and gave each other hands slaps, celebrating the moment that was theirs. "This was something for us and nobody else. It marks the wildest night that four friends ever had. It came, and it went, and anyone who we tell will think we're crazy. So, let's never tell anyone about it. It's a bond, my friends," said Victor. The others were at a loss for words, but they understood what Victor meant.

Walking back to the car, a big, loud, glowing bus drove past them at a furious speed. It was heading in the same direction that they were going, transporting people who traveled far for work. It was covered in all sorts of bright lights of different colors in order to make itself visible to other cars on the overnight trip. "We have to follow that bus. It can lead the way; then you won't have to guess where the road curves," Jorge told Thomas.

Victor agreed. "Don't let it get away." They got into the car and caught up to the ridiculous-looking bus that was full of poor indigenous workers who had to report to their low-wage, indentured jobs at the earliest hours of the morning.

Fortunately, the monstrous calamity lit up the road and gave Thomas peace of mind that he wasn't going to drive off a cliff. He remained a safe distance behind it just in case something went terribly wrong and he had to react immediately. He considered it a blessing that the bus appeared when it did because his mind was almost too distracted to focus. It was still in the process of digesting what they'd just seen.

In the back seat of the car, Victor was reviewing the footage he caught with his cell phone camera. He was able to take two videos that were each three minutes long. Both videos were similar, showing a glowing object that floated steadily in the sky. He and

Chavez examined every detail of the image, but both remained inconclusive as to what it was. It didn't have any doors or any windows, nor were there any particulars that suggested it had been manufactured.

"This is like something out of a science fiction movie. I don't think it's from this planet," said Chavez.

Jorge was nervous and uneasy. He couldn't stop fidgeting. The more he thought of the UFO, the more of an impact it had on him. He rolled down the window and smoked a cigarette to calm his nerves.

"What's wrong with you?" asked Thomas catching the edge of his friend's uneasiness.

"I don't know. I'm just tired of being in this loud ass car. I want to get to the lake and get some sleep," he replied before letting out a loud yawn. "I just don't know anymore," he said.

"What don't you know, Jorge?" asked Chavez. "Anything!" exclaimed Jorge in frustration. "Fuck, we just saw proof of extra-terrestrial life. Doesn't that mess up every notion and theory that you have ever had about the world?" The question was followed by silence inside the car. It was too soon for such a question. It wouldn't be good if any of them decided to have a mental breakdown in the car in the middle of nowhere.

"Just smoke this, and you'll be fine," said Thomas as he handed Jorge a pipe packed with Oaxaca. Everyone was exhausted and reverted quietly to thinking about the UFO and the rest of the evening's events in their own way.

Thomas' eyes were in need of rest. He couldn't stop yawning, and his neck was stiff from all the tension. Chavez and Victor had already fallen asleep while Jorge continued playing DJ. At the same time, he kept an eye out for the exit because they were close.

The sun began to make its initial mark on the night sky. The bus had led the way for nearly 45 minutes. It signaled to pull into a gas station to refuel for the remainder of its journey. Thomas gave the bus one last look as they drove past it and noticed the words that were painted on the side, which read, "Dios es tu Guilla." Thomas smiled, looked at himself in the rearview mirror, and continued towards the lake. Ten minutes later, Jorge saw a large white sign that read, 'Bienvenidos a Sololá.'

"There it is," he told Thomas, who was relieved to see that they were finally there.

Chapter Six
Panajachel and the Soul

Outside of a mangled shack that stood behind a little school in Panajachel, a little unbathed boy pondered where to find breakfast for himself and his sister. Seven-year-old Leopoldo and three-year-old Gloria were left to fend for survival since the day their mother died from Cholera. The woman suffered unbearable weakness and pain for days until her dehydrated body could no longer fight the parasite. She died with Leopoldo sitting next to her as he held his baby sister in his arms. The decomposing corpse was found four days later in the room. By that time, Leopoldo had already left his baby sister to start a new life.

It was too early in the morning to dip into his regular food sources. The local housemaids were off duty for the weekend, and the tourists were still sleeping comfortably in their white linens at one of the local hotels. Leopoldo would often cling to a group of tourists for the day and offer his services as a guide while also serenading them with ranchero love ballads for tips. He liked being around tourists. He believed that they were special because they had money, food, and all God's blessings. At such an early age, Leopoldo had already developed a skewed vision of the world. He believed that God didn't like poor people and that he and his sister were being punished. They often spent time by the church courtyard, praying for forgiveness. After that, they would sit end wait for mass goers to arrive in order to beg them for money or morsel and food.

Little Gloria's life perspective was silently growing as well. Her speech was developing poorly for a three-year-old. She hardly spoke a sound, but she was bright. She looked out for her older brother and supported all his clever ideas. Her crystal green eyes were always wide open and alert, equipping her with cognitive wit and rationality. She had long blonde hair that was rarely washed and had never been brushed. She walked around with her sort cheeks stained with dirt and food remnants from her last meal. To her, the world was a confusing place, but her brother's presence always provided the emotional comfort she needed. Gloria followed Leopoldo everywhere he went and rarely cried or complained.

Leopoldo sat on the street curbside thinking long and hard about a place to find food. Gloria sat patiently on the sidewalk behind her brother, staring at a scruffy black mutt that was heeded towards the lake for food. The image sparked an idea in her mind. She remembered that the water taxi brought in fresh *Pitaya fruit* on Saturdays from a farm across the lake. She went over to Leopoldo and said, "Agua, aya!" as she pointed to the lake.

Leopoldo looked into her big eyes and knew that she was thinking about the weekend fruit delivery. He stood up, grabbed little sister by the hand, and headed toward the lake.

Somewhere else along that lake, sunlight entered the Lancer and pierced through Thomas' eyelids. He turned his head to the left and noticed something cotton rubbing against his forehead. It was the sock on Chavez's left foot.

"Get your foot out of my face," said Thomas in a groggy voice. He slowly opened his heavy eyes to see where they were. Nothing looked familiar. Thomas rubbed his hands on his face. He looked around the car and observed the snoring aftermath from the night before. Their limbs were stretched from end to end. Jorge's feet hung out the window while Victor's feet were both placed comfortably on top of the car's center console. Thomas' movement awoke Jorge.

"C'mon Flores, go back to sleep," he said.

"Hey Jorge, what the hell happened had night?" asked Thomas. Jorge gave himself a good stretch before anything else. "I have no idea. That shit seemed like something out of a movie. It doesn't stop playing over and over in my head."

One by one, they all woke up and got out of the car. Victor opened the car door and put both his feet on the curb. His entire leg had fallen asleep. He stomped his right foot up and down in order to relieve the numbness. Thomas took notice of the lakefront carpentry business.

The townspeople were up, performing their morning routines to set up business for the day. Two indigenous women walked down the road with an oversized basket of tortillas and other baked goods on their heads. An old, shirtless man with a heavy gray mustache walked out from an efficiency within the outdoor carpentry. He leaned over a stone washbasin to clean his face, neck, and armpits with an orange rag that was hanging off a tree branch.

"Why don't we go down to the central road and find a place to eat?" suggested Jorge. Thomas turned the key in the ignition, which alarmed some of the locals. He drove down *Calle de la Playa* and turned right onto Calle Rancho Grande.

Jorge told Thomas to park his car across the street from a small, quaint hotel. Jorge wanted to find a place where they could leave the car without any problem. The two guards standing outside the hotel gave the Lancer a stern look of suspicion. They were also hung over, which may have intensified the stare even more. Thomas turned off the car, and the guards walked towards them. They both wore a t-shirt, jeans, leather boots, and a hunting vest where the guns were stored.

"Parking isn't allowed here," said the first guard in a firm voice.

"We drove in last night from the capital to see a friend. Do you know if the Ramon family owns this hotel?" asked Jorge. The men grew even more suspicious when they saw four male strangers asking for their employer.

"Who's asking?" said the heavy-set guard.

"Jorge Palma; I'm a friend of Monica Ramon from Guatemala and..." he pointed at Thomas, "...he studies dentistry with her at Universidad Marroquin." Monica Ramon was the third wheel in the group of girlfriends that consisted of Karen, Helga, and her. Monica was from Panajachel. Her parents owned a hotel near the lake.

"This is Monica's hotel. What's it called?" asked Thomas.

"Villa Lago," said Jorge while the two guards whispered to each other. They were doing their job, which was to protect the hotel, the owners, and its customers. "We just wanted to know if we could park our car in front of the hotel without a problem because we want to take the boat taxi over to San Pedro for the day. Monica told us that if we ever needed anything while in Pana, come to the hotel," said Jorge.

The guards stepped away to make a phone call. In Guatemala, crime didn't have a face, so the guards had to take all the necessary precautions before disclosing any information. The second guard stepped out and asked Jorge to provide their names with identification.

"*Jorge Palma y Thomas Flores,*" he replied before handing the guard their licenses. He returned to the office to inform guard number one, who was talking on the phone with Monica's mother. They had to be reached on her cell phone because the Ramon family was vacationing in Rio Dulce. She recognized both names and advised the guards to let the young men park in the private lot. The guards came out with their IDs and handed them back to Jorge. Thomas put the transmission in reverse, backing up the car about fifty feet into the gated area. Everyone was grateful for the favor, thanking the guards for their hospitality before locking the car and heading off on foot.

Time froze during the early hours in Panajachel. The outside world was forgotten, and the only thing left to do was blend into the tranquility of peaceful living. They were miles away from their debilitating insecurities, their fear of failure, the pressures of love, life's confusions, and from the pain of reality. In Panajachel, humans are free to live as they are meant to live, peacefully and in thought.

The streets were full of small businesses, restaurants, and charming hotels. There weren't any moving cars, only a few that were parked along the road. People were free to roam the streets without any fear of getting run over. All of the eateries had banners promoting beer and drink specials. There were menus and daily specials posted on decorative signs.

Chavez and Jorge were low on funds, and they worried about the burden of asking Thomas or Victor to pay for breakfast. They each had enough money for the boat ride fee and a meal in San

Pedro. Whenever Thomas or Victor would see a restaurant they liked, Jorge would suggest they look for another place. He mentioned they get a typical Guatemalan breakfast, which consists of eggs, black beans, cheese, tortilla, a side of homemade sour cream, and coffee. He also knew that it was the cheapest meal they'd find anywhere.

To Jorge's luck, they walked in front of a small outdoor shopping center where a young indigenous girl was setting out some chairs in the courtyard. The sign in the front said *'Desayuno Tipico: ocho quetzals'*. Thomas, being from the United States, was a bit skeptical about the quality of food that one received for the equivalent of one US dollar.

"Are you guys sure we should be eating here?" asked Thomas.

"Of course; why not?" responded Jorge.

The young waitress came back to the table and asked, "Would you like anything to drink?"

There weren't any menus, so Jorge asked, "What do you have to drink?"

The girl paused for a minute to think.

"We have orange juice and coffee, and I think we might have orchata left," she said as she looked back at the kitchen to see if anything else came to mind.

"And what's there to eat?" asked Chavez as though he was going to get something other than the special. "We have el desayuno tipico, fruit, aaaand bread."

She stressed the 'and' because she couldn't think of anything else the restaurant could serve. Low-budget eateries in Guatemala were always honest about their modesty. This place was no exception.

"We'll all have el tipico," said Jorge. The waitress went back through the swinging screened door that led to the kitchen.

Thomas, Jorge, Chavez, and Victor sat around the table, peacefully absorbing the soothing sounds of the Panajachel sunrise. Their minds were temporarily hypnotized by the calmness of Panajachel. The soft colors of the morning and the harmonized sound of the birds revitalized their sanity. Neither of them mentioned the flying object in the sky, but they were all thinking about it. So much so that, they didn't talk about anything else that had occurred the previous night. They just sat in silence, trying to make sense of it all.

The guys were famished beyond belief when the food finally came. It didn't take long for them to devour everything in sight. They enjoyed every last drop and paid the bill.

"We have to get to the lake. I'm not sure what time the next water taxi gets here," said Jorge.

They walked towards the lake and came to a flight of stairs that led to a shoreside souvenir market. The merchants sold costume jewelry, pipes, knives, and other items made of wood and stone. Chavez and Jorge noticed the assortment of smoking pipes. They walked over to the tables to see if there was anything worth buying.

Thomas was checking his missed calls and text messages. There was one missed call from his mother and a text message from Mercedes: [I'm going to be alone today after my volleyball game. Come over because I need to tell you something,] Thomas ignored the message and called his mother long distance. There was a two-hour difference, but he was sure that his parents were already awake, doing their morning routine, getting ready for work.

She picked up the phone by saying, "Good morning, Dr.Flores's office." Saturday was always the most profitable day of the work week for his parents.

"Hi, Mom," he said in a low voice.

"Hey, it's good to finally hear from you. Did you forget that you have parents?" She said.

"No, sorry I didn't call last night. I was at a concert. How's it going at the clinic?" he asked.

"Fine. Thank God your father had a few big cases this week. Later we're going out for dinner with your brothers and the babies," she said. Thomas regretted the fact that he wasn't around to see his nieces grow up. He felt that he was losing out on the best years of his family's history.

It wasn't long before the conversation became uncomfortable for Thomas. His mother started asking about the cost of his new dental instruments.

"I spent four hundred dollars on your card," he mumbled, but she understood. Still, he felt guilty that they were wasting their hard-earned money on him. It didn't help the fact that she never fell short of reminding him how expensive everything was.

"Well, make sure they last as long as possible. Your father and I are still paying off our debt from the mess with the other clinic."

"Aren't you married to a dentist?" he asked jokingly.

"These days, there are hardly any patients. The economic crisis has affected everyone, and your father doesn't have as much work as before," she replied to make him understand the seriousness of the situation.

"Well, I have to go; it's getting busy. I'll call you later," said his mother.

"Okay, love you, Mom," he said.

Victor approached a vendor's table where handmade scarves were being sold. The woven fabric was designed with representative colors and patterns from the surrounding pueblos.

"That one is very beautiful. I think your girlfriend would like it," said the vendor. She was an old, indigenous woman dressed in a traditional green and purple Mayan dress. Her hair was long and black, and her anterior incisors were capped with gold crowns and amalgamated. "I also have these over here and some others in the back," she said while emphasizing her other products.

Each bright color softened the stubbornness in his heart. They reminded him of Kayla, who was a fashionista. He knew that she was right about everything. The entire evening led Victor to an obvious realization. He started to understand how lucky he was to have Kayla in his life and that being loved was something that shouldn't be taken for granted. He thought a gift would be a kind gesture to start apologizing. Victor bought two scarves from the vendor for thirty quetzals.

Just as he had put his money in his wallet, two children approached Victor to ask him for money. They wore rags, and their feet were bare. The little boy tugged on Victor's shirt, catching him by surprise. Victor looked down at the child.

"Oye, Junior, where did you come from?"

The boy was anything but shy. "I went to the lake to see if Don Ramos had fruit for my sister and me, but Señora Magda told me that he was having motor problems since Wednesday and probably wasn't going to come today," he said.

"So, who gave that to her?" asked Victor while looking at Gloria happily eating her fruit. He was amused by the children.

"Señora Magda, she had some in her bag," the boy responded.

"So why are you here?" asked Victor.

"Because Señora Magda only had one, and I gave it to my little sister, but the shop sells a bag of chips for one quetzal, and I don't have enough money to buy it," replied the boy.

Thomas noticed Victor talking to the kid and walked over to see what the discussion was about.

"What happened?" he asked.

"This kid wants money to buy a bag of chips at the store," said Victor in a way that made it sound like he wasn't going to give the kid the money, though he fully intended to. Thomas instantly caught on to the prank.

"What are you going to do for us?"

Leopoldo crossed his arms and thought of ways to earn their money.

Over by the pipes, Jorge and Chavez were discussing the potential colors of a particular one they were admiring. "I think it's going to be blue with yellow stripes, said Chavez. The vendor was a lost American who found his peace within the concealed jungles of Guatemala. He earned a modest living by selling pipes and hemp products in the Panajachel market. He was a shirtless hippy who wore cargo pants, sandals, and a collection of friendship bracelets on his wrist. He also had massive dreadlocks and a scruffy beard that was in serious need of washing. There were many social refugees like him who settled around Guatemala. There, they found a place of meditation, away from modern distractions that disallowed true appreciation for the beauties of life. Panajachel offered the opportunity to detach oneself completely from the rest of the world. All too often, the detachment became permanent.

Jorge found a dragon-shaped pipe that he liked. Chavez took a good look at it as well and agreed on its unique attractiveness.

"Yeah, this is a nice one. Hey Thomas, come look at this," said Jorge before turning around to find him and Victor talking to two little kids. Leopoldo was on his hands and knees while Gloria stood on his back, mumbling a church song and clapping to the beat. They were entertaining for money.

Thomas looked at the piece of glass in his buddy's hands. He thought it was a steal for the price. Still, Jorge knew that he could haggle the price down even more.

"Give it to me for sixty Q," he asked to start the bidding. His offering price was bold, but Jorge knew that he'd be one of a handful of people to buy something from the vendor that day, which gave him a bargaining advantage.

"One hundred is the best I can do. I wish I could help you, but I don't make the pipes; I just sell them," said the vendor.

"Sixty, and I'll take it right now?" It was Jorge's final offer.

"No, I'm sorry. I can't sell it to you for that price," repeated the vendor.

Jorge put the pipe down and began to walk away. He'd barely made it a few steps when the vendor called him back.

"Okay, you can take it for sixty." They walked right back to the table to complete the transaction.

Thomas wanted to see if the guy sold weed.

"You have anything else to sell?" he asked.

The hippy studied Thomas for a second before answering. "Something for the pipe?" he asked.

Thomas nodded his head

"Follow me," said the hippy.

The four of them walked behind the table, where they weren't as exposed to the public. The hippy opened the drawer of an old wooden nightstand where he stored his personal stash of weed. He wasn't necessarily a drug dealer, but he always kept a little extra just in case he came across any inquiring tourists. He pulled out some immature weed that was wrapped in old newspaper. No one was impressed with what they saw.

"Is this the best that you have?" asked Thomas with a look of disappointment. It was skunkweed. The leaves were dry, and it was filled with stems and undeveloped seeds. It wasn't the type of weed that one expected to find at the lake. Chavez put it up to his nose to smell the quality. He confirmed that it was garbage weed, dry with stems and undeveloped seeds.

"You can find better weed in San Pedro," he said.

"I'll sell you a half-ounce for one hundred quetzals," offered the hippy.

Thomas laughed in his face. They didn't want to waste that much money on junk weed.

"It's better if we buy weed in San Pedro," said Jorge.

"Are you sure we can get some there?" asked Thomas.

"Ahuevos, there's an old man that lives up in the mountain who sells some good Oaxaca," replied Jorge.

They left with only the pipe and found Victor still being entertained by the little beggars. The young boy was singing a vintage ranchero song by Vincente Fernandez:

Hablando de mujeres y traciones,

Se fueron consumiendo las botellas...

Leopoldo had the four men hanging on to every one of his words. The child had just reminded them of the crushing power that women had over men. They had all felt it at some point in their lives. Like most men, their pain was hidden behind a chauvinistic and emotionless cocoon that prevented weakness and vulnerability in front of others.

Jorge approached the little singer and asked him for his name.

"Leopoldo, and this is my little sister, Gloria," he said while pointing to the baby girl who had fruit chunks on her face.

"Look, we need to get to San Pedro. Do you know which boat can take us there?" asked Jorge, who trusted the little boy's street smarts.

"The one at the pier; follow me, and I'll show you," said Leopoldo, who was excited to help the four strangers.

Before they left, Thomas went to a small café and bought each child a ham and cheese baguette and orange juice.

They walked to the shoreline, where Thomas and Victor were met by one of the natural wonders of the world. They were looking at an enormous water-filled gorge created over eighty thousand years ago through volcanic eruptions. The most awe-inspiring features of the lake were the three natural wonders that aligned its southern flank. They were the volcanoes of San Pedro, Toliman, and Atitlan. The immense volcanoes looked as though they had sprung from the bottom of the lake. It was truly a sight that elevated the spirit.

The high mountain winds moved the deep blue water, creating a steady current that ran toward the shore. Thomas noticed early-morning fishing boats skimming the water for what he assumed was bass. The rest of the shore seemed relatively uninhabited, much like the way it looked in ancient times.

"How deep is it?" asked Thomas.

"No one knows because the bottom has yet to be reached. This country holds the secrets to the earth's past. There's no other place that's so uniquely diversified from border to border," said Jorge with pride. Jorge's connection with Guatemala's natural splendor formed the basis of his conceptual thinking. He adored his country. The spirit of Guatemala followed him everywhere he went.

They followed Leopoldo around the shoreline and towards the pier. They stepped through the series of dips on the rocky dirt path.

The pier wasn't far away, and they all maintained a steady pace, one behind the other, carefully preventing injury.

The sun pierced the skin on their necks. Jorge and Thomas took off their shirts to let the breeze cool off their skin. They walked up to a tree that had its roots growing into the shallow water. It provided a nice shade. From there, Jorge could see that there weren't any boats at the pier, only a couple of indigenous girls who were cooling off with a dip in the water.

"Leopoldo, go to the pier with your sister and tell us when the boat arrives," he said to the boy. In actuality, he was just getting rid of them because he thought it was a nice place to have a morning smoke session with the new pipe. It was a relaxing place to take a break under the shade and enjoy the view from the water's edge. The kids scampered off like they were told.

Jorge sat on a large tree root that went out about twenty feet into the lake. He packed his new pipe with some weed while the others found a comfortable place to sit. Thomas climbed up the tree and settled himself on a sturdy branch that hung over the shallow water. Chavez also found a branch on the tree where he could sit and roll a joint.

Under that tree, with the sounds of a light breeze dancing over the water, they were absent from time and closer to reality. The entire night of reckless debauchery couldn't have had a better ending; for as far as they knew, their little adventure had no more surprises.

It wasn't long before the inevitable happened. They each started to think about the UFO. The thought hadn't stopped lingering in the back of their minds. Thomas didn't want to remain silent about the event any longer.

"What the fuck did we see last night?" he asked. Jorge looked up at him. "Who knows? I've been thinking about it, and nothing makes sense; it had to be some type of government experiment."

Thomas disagreed in part with Jorge's explanation.

"I don't think Guatemala's government could afford something like that." Chavez agreed.

"Ahuevos, Guatemala doesn't do things like that; something so sophisticated like the thing we saw last night would cost way more than this country can afford." Chavez took off his hat and rubbed his hands through his curly fro. "I don't think any country on this planet can afford to build something like that." He took a hit of the joint and then passed it down to Victor.

"Shit, I don't even know if I should smoke this again. The last time I did it, I saw a UFO flying over my head," said Victor to make the others laugh. He wasn't thinking too heavily about the flying entity. To him, it was something that happened and was probably never going to happen again.

Though difficult to admit, the others accepted that they'd seen something majestic. Chavez, Thomas, and Jorge didn't need too much convincing to know that they'd seen a UFO.

"That shit was so real," said Jorge.

"Yeah, but do you really think it was alien?" asked Chavez. He referred to beings from another planet.

"I do. Nothing that any of us have ever seen suggests that it was from the earth; nothing on television, nothing on the news, nothing in our cities, nothing," said Thomas.

"It's the beginning of the space battle. The aliens are going to enslave the men and reproduce with our women," blurted Victor to lighten up the mood left by Thomas' dramatic statement.

"What the hell are Aliens doing in Guatemala?" asked Jorge as he took a hit.

"It's a sign of the end of the world. All sorts of crazy things are going to happen from here on out," said Chavez.

"Crazy things like this?" asked Victor as he held up his cell phone to show Chavez one of the pictures he had taken of the flying object. The evidence didn't lie. It was a flashing fireball radiating in vivid sheerness.

Then they heard a voice yelling their way. It was Leopoldo, running towards them as fast as he could. "The boat is coming! The boat is coming!" They all looked out to the water and noticed the vessel heading back at high speed. They finished the joint and went to the pier.

The boat had already docked by the time they got to the pier. There was a lot of cargo that needed to be moved before the next trip. The citizens of the lake worked in unity, moving products on and off the boat. Unfortunately, they didn't have the resources to help them improve their back-breaking methods. That didn't stop them from working as one. Even Leopoldo was lending a hand by carrying an elderly woman's basket of tamales onto land. Little Gloria helped as well by carrying the elderly woman's sweater that she accidentally dropped on the pier when stepping off the boat.

Thomas walked to the far end of the pier and took a picture of himself with the volcano as the backdrop. He took a minute to admire the magnificent site that surrounded him from all angles. Thomas looked down and saw his reflection in the crystal water.

He felt like he was being pulled towards it.

Then he noticed small fish swimming under the pier. He got on his knees and dipped his head under the structure to see where the fish went. There were hundreds of them slowly swimming in place under the shaded area. He ran his hand through the cool water, and they all scattered.

Thomas was left with the urge to take off his clothes and jump in the water, but he didn't know how long until the boat departed. He saw that his friends were lingering around the pier and that there was still plenty of cargo to move. Thomas knew it wasn't a moment to waste. The temptation was too much to bear.

He removed his shoes and socks and then noticed something written on one of the pier beams. In black marker, it read, *"Somos esclavos de ayer, pero somos los dueños de mañana."* The thick and curvy penmanship led Thomas to assume it was written by a young girl, probably one of the ones he saw earlier swimming off the pier. The words were a testament to the philosophical intelligence and analytical rationalization of Guatemala's natives. Thomas then proceeded to take off his pants and run off the pier without hesitation. He jumped as far as he could, diving like a torpedo into Lake Atitlan. The ancient water revitalized every cell of his body, cleansing his spirit and his soul.

Meanwhile, Jorge and Chavez were waiting to get the captain's attention. They were trying to find out the cost of the boat ride. It wasn't an easy task with everything else that was happening. Fortunately, they were with Leopoldo, who got the attention of the captain's assistant. He was also a young boy, no older than twelve years old, probably the captain's son.

"My four friends want to get to San Pedro," said Leopoldo.

"Tell them thirty quetzals for the trip," replied the assistant as he counted the corn crates. Leopoldo and his sister would ride for free because they were considered guides. It was a common practice among the poor children of the lake to tag along with a group of tourists in hopes of receiving some form of payment.

Thomas' dip was brief but well worth it. He got out of the water and put on his clothes without drying his body. Jorge whistled to alert Thomas that they were getting on the boat. Thomas took another look at the quote that was written on the pier and smiled. He felt different, as though a huge weight had been lifted off of his shoulders. Thomas was no longer worried about the future; he just wanted to live in the present and find whatever he was meant to find.

One by one, they stepped into the turquoise-painted wooden boat. It was long and old, with seven rows of wood planks where riders could sit. Over their heads was a low roof made of blue tarp and sticks for storage and protection from the rain and sun. At first, it seemed that there weren't going to be many people on the boat ride to San Pedro. Apart from the four adventures and their little guides, there were only two other women on the boat. Still, the boat didn't move. Thomas couldn't figure out the delay until he noticed a group of ten people walking down the mountain's edge, carrying all sorts of items, light and heavy. They were running late because a rain storm from the previous week left mudslide remnants along their normal bus route.

The water taxi was the primary means of transportation for the people who lived around the lake. Their schedule was simple: know when the taxi came and when the taxi left. They would have to travel from far distances before taking the water taxi to another part of the lake where they worked. The daily process was grueling but necessary. They endured daily hardship because it was the only way to make money and feed their families.

The indigenous natives arrived on the boat and unloaded their items on the deck. Some had bags, while others had sacks of food. One man had tools. A young mother with four children unloaded a giant basket of tortillas that she carried on her head the entire way from the bus stop. They all stepped onto the boat with the help of the young skipper. He lent his hands to every man, woman, and child that got on so that they wouldn't slip or fall.

The women wore traditional Mayan dresses, and they spoke Cankjobal. It was a native language that had survived thousands of years. Thomas tried deciphering their dialect, but he found it impossible.

Suddenly, the boat was full. The four friends found themselves inching closer to one another in order to make room for all the passengers. Once they were all tightly packed together, the boat docked off the pier and headed towards the open lake.

Thomas and Jorge sat on the first row, while Victor and Chavez sat on the second row. Leopoldo and his little sister Gloria sat on a small bench at the front of the boat with the other workers. A mother with two little girls sat next to Jorge. He noticed how young she was and felt sympathy for the poor girl. She looked impossibly young, like she was still a teenager.

The water was choppy, and the boats' velocity created a misty breeze that sprayed through the air. The boat skimmed the waves and rode against the current, jumping every time it hit a wave. There were three stops before San Pedro, which gave the four adventurers plenty of time to absorb the raw essence of the lake.

Every town along the lakeshore was named after one of the twelve Disciples of Christ. They were named by the early Spanish settlers who arrived in Panajachel to spread Christianity. The first stop was San Jose Chacaya. The boat slowly docked next to a small pier, where a few of the passengers got off with their belongings before disappearing into the jungle. Thomas was confused; it didn't look like there was anywhere for them to go. All he saw was a dense collection of trees and wild grass. Once everyone was off, the boat slowly pulled out west, onward to the next stop.

Jorge couldn't help but focus on the injustice and neglect that the locals had to endure. They were the forgotten and mistreated victims of a political system that didn't recognize their worth and potential. Jorge struggled to accept their living conditions and the hardships they had to endure without any of the conveniences that modern society took for granted. Instead, they were driven to survive by the spirit of the earth.

Jorge felt someone tap on his shoulder. It was an old man. He had sliced pieces of avocado and was sharing with anyone that wanted. Jorge and Thomas graciously took a piece from the kind stranger. Victor and Chavez graciously denied it. The act was a testament to the lake's purity, of the people's generosity and innocence.

Jorge drifted into his own stream of thought. Panajachel had a way of bringing him back to his roots. It made him think of the direction he wanted to take his life. He knew that the success of the country started and ended with the millions of natives who thirsted for an opportunity to better their living conditions. It was his dream to help bring them out of poverty and into a prosperous future, to a place where they would always be recognized as human beings.

San Marcos was another desolate location. There wasn't even a pier, just a wooden board that prevented anyone from having to walk in the water. The majority of the passengers got off at San Marcos. Once again, the assistant helped to get each person and their items onto the shore. The young mother gathered her belongings and stepped off the boat with her daughters. Thomas and Jorge both lingered in the thought of her unfortunate reality as she walked into the wild jungle, holding a swaddled baby around her neck, a toddler by the hand, and a basket of items on her head.

San Juan de la Laguna was the final stop before San Pedro. It was a small town with a population of only a few thousand, but it was one of the most active tourist destinations along the lake. The boat approached a lively hotel with a bar and pool. An American couple exited the boat. After that, only the four friends remained.

It would take nearly a half hour to ride from San Juan to San Pedro. Thomas, Jorge, Chavez, and Victor took the opportunity to rest their heads wherever they found room. They were running on little sleep, and it seemed like a good opportunity to rest before the next part of the adventure. Looking up at the blue carp and listening to the sound of the running engine, Thomas closed his eyes and floated away a little farther.

He woke up in another realm, far away from Guatemala. Thomas was standing in the living room of his grandparent's house, which had been destroyed by Hurricane Katrina. Everything was just as he remembered from his childhood. All the furniture in the living room was set up exactly the way it was when he was little. Thomas walked around the living room and looked at the family pictures that hung on the wall. It produced a warm feeling in his heart to be back at the place where he had made so many great memories. Then he heard his grandmother call his name.

"Thomas, Thomas!" Thomas turned around and saw her sitting on the leather couch with his older brother. They both welcomed him, and he sat on the couch. His grandmother basked, "How are you? How's school going?" He didn't get the chance to answer.

They heard the doorbell ring. Thomas' grandmother stood up to see who it was. To everyone's delight, his grandfather walked into the house. He looked youthful and strong, unlike the final days of his life when he was weak and suffering from kidney failure.

"Papa, it's so good to see you. I thought I would never see you again," said Thomas.

"I'm here, and I feel good," said his grandfather as he placed his keys on the key holder that had always been next to the front door.

They all walked to the kitchen, where he sat at his usual place at the dinner table. Grandmother served dinner while Thomas and his brother caught up with Grandfather about everything going on in their lives. His grandmother was so happy to have her beloved husband in the house again that she briefly stopped cooking to hold back tears of joy. She cooked all of his favorite meals, one after the other.

And then, Thomas' grandfather stood up from the table and said, "It's time for me to go. I wanted to see everyone one last time." Thomas was like a confused little boy. He couldn't understand why his grandfather would leave.

"Papa, don't leave us again. We all need you here with us. Nothing is the same since you left."

His grandfather turned and said to him, "I have to go; take care of your grandmother for me."

He walked outside and stepped into a blue Gran Torino that was in perfect condition. Thomas ran out after him and noticed a small child dressed in a white baptism outfit sitting in the passenger seat. The child had blue eyes and curly blonde hair. He looked like a little angel.

As the car engine turned on, Thomas yelled, "Papa, Papa, don't leave us; we want you to stay!" Thomas' grandfather rolled down the window to give him one last piece of advice.

"Don't be scared. I'm always going to be with you. I love you all very much." The windows to the car rolled up, and Thomas watched as it drove down the street into a white light. He waved goodbye, doing his best to control the tears.

Thomas opened his eyes and saw Chavez standing above him, trying to get his attention.

"Thomas, Thomas, we're here."

Thomas woke up and wiped the tears from his eyes. The deep sleep left him a bit puzzled and groggy. He sat up and remembered every detail from his dream. Everything felt so intimate and real. It was as though his grandfather had reached out to him at a moment when he needed it most.

Chapter Seven
San Pedro

The four friends walked off the pier and onto a steep walkway. Leopoldo and Gloria stayed behind to help around the dock.

"We'll see you two later," said Jorge as they walked up a little street to find something to eat. San Pedro was well known for having a variety of restaurants that catered to the pot smoker's palate. Thomas was excited to go into the first place he saw and smoke freely in the ambiance.

"Let's go eat here. What do you think, Jorge?" he asked. He pointed at a pier-side bar.

"This place looks good. But why don't we walk a little more to see what else there is," replied Jorge. He had a few places in mind that he knew were worth the wait.

Victor focused on making a phone call. His efforts were useless because of the weak cell phone signal in San Pedro. He wanted to call Kayla and tell her that he was fine. He felt it was the right thing to do because she loved him and was probably concerned about his whereabouts. Everything from the night before brought Victor to a rational realization about his life. He was starting to understand a genuine rule of nature that he'd previously neglected to acknowledge. It was that life moved a lot faster than most people were willing to accept, including himself. Kayla offered him something that was worth trying to preserve and hold on to. Victor didn't want her to become nothing but a memory that faded with time.

It was a perfect day in San Pedro. The sky cleared the way for the sun, dispersing the clouds towards the south behind the magnificent volcanoes. There were different types of businesses on every corner; a tourist office, a souvenir shop, a café that offered fresh coffee made from the beans grown in Xela, and a burger joint.

"Hey Chavez, which way to the weed?" asked Jorge.

Chavez was the only one who remembered where the drug dealer's house was.

"It's up that road," he said while pointing in the northern direction.

"How do you even know that he is here?" asked

'Thomas, who didn't feel like going on another wild goose chase.

"I don't. The last time I went there, some housemaid sold me the weed. I've never seen the pot dealer, but I hear that he's a crazy old man," he explained.

Jorge led them to a small café that had *Relax San Pedro* painted on the front door. The cantina-style restaurant was empty, with no guests or servers in sight. Thomas stepped into the little souvenir shop and noticed the different wood carvings displayed on the wall; some were replications of Mayan artifacts, and some were of jungle animals. There were plenty of Christian-themed decorations as well.

It appeared as though no one was working. Jorge was about to suggest they leave when a young girl walked out from the back.

"Good morning. Do you prefer sitting here or out by the lake?"

she asked.

"By the lake is fine," replied Jorge.

She took them to an area that was more pleasant than Jorge could ever describe. The wicker patio set was situated lakeside. Jorge and Victor took the single chairs while Chavez and Thomas sunk their bodies into the loveseat's cushion. The awe-inspiring view deserved a silent moment of recognition. The earth-green mountains formed a great wall that kept separated San Pedro from the rest of the world. It was all a testament to the simplistic beauty of life.

The people of San Pedro relied daily on the precious lake for their basic needs. It was the nucleus of their society. Thomas noticed children bathing in the freshwater. They dove into the water and washed their bodies with homemade soap. Meanwhile, their mothers were washing clothes with the same soap. The naturalness of everything made Thomas feel unworthy of invading their peace. It made him understand how much he took life for granted.

"This is beautiful," said Jorge, knowing the others would agree with what he was saying. Thomas couldn't believe where he was, where his destiny had taken him. He wondered if his insecurities were necessary to burden. Nature was telling him no. It was telling him that life wasn't meant to be so complicated.

"You were right, Jorge. It was all worth it," he said. The waitress came out with glasses of water and four menus. They were all anxious to have a celebratory meal in the tranquil setting. Jorge reached into his pocket and pulled out a joint that had been stored away for that exact moment.

At first, Thomas was nervous that they'd get in trouble. He wasn't used to getting high in a public establishment. "Are you sure we can do this?" he asked Jorge. "You have to learn to be less tense," replied Jorge as he searched his pockets for the lighter.

The waitress came back and served them coffee before taking their orders. Jorge lit the marijuana cigarette and took a hit in front of the young lady's face. Thomas looked at her to see a reaction. There was none. She couldn't have cared any less that they were getting high. That was when Thomas realized that he was at a place where weed was socially accepted without scrutiny or persecution. It was the most freedom that he'd ever felt.

To the surprise of everyone but Jorge, the menu offered a wide variety of selections. Thomas expected to see typical Guatemalan food being offered; frijoles, tamales, meat, or chicken with vegetables. That wasn't the case. The menu had all sorts of different things to eat.

"Where are the owners of the restaurant from?" asked Thomas. He noticed an international selection of meals available.

"I think they're from Switzerland," replied the waitress.

"That explains the fondue on the menu. Do they live here in San Pedro?" he asked.

"They only come here a few months out of the year," she replied.

"Ah, well, at least they leave a good menu and kind workers to attend to the clients," he replied. The waitress smiled.

"I'll be back to take your order when you're ready," she said.

They continued to smoke the last of the weed while the young waitress prepared a basket of assorted coffee breads. Then, Jorge spoke.

"Man, I want to fuck her," he said with lazy, bloodshot eyes. They could all see her through a window.

"Poor girl, leave her alone," said Thomas. He found Jorge's honesty to be humorous but wasn't himself in such a mood.

Jorge was a little shocked to hear Thomas' sudden change in morality.

"Look who's talking," he said. Thomas looked directly into Jorge's eyes to see where his words were going. "You ordered me and Chavez our first escort from Puchis; you're one of the sickest minds I know," reminded Jorge.

Chavez laughed as he, too, recalled the day.

"Yeah, but those were professional whores. This girl doesn't deserve a group of stoned-out degenerates undressing her with their eyes," said Thomas.

"I don't know," said Victor as he turned his head to get a better look at the girl. "She looks like she knows how to handle a big dick," he added while creating an animated description with his hand and mouth to demonstrate exactly what he was talking about.

Thomas felt like he'd put himself on the spot but didn't hesitate to continue with his explanation. "I just feel like I need to concentrate more on the important things of life instead of stupid shit like drinking, smoking, and fucking. I need to focus."

Jorge didn't see the need for such a dramatic conclusion. "But you're doing fine. What's wrong with having a little fun in between?" he asked.

"I just need to stop having this much fun. It's causing me to become less focused on my goals. I don't deserve any of this," said Thomas before taking a sip of coffee.

"Look at everything that we went through last night. Those things don't happen to just anyone. And if you'd been home studying or jerking your dick, you would've missed it all," said Jorge.

"Perhaps, maybe it was meant to be, or maybe it wasn't. I just don't want to spend the rest of my life chasing wild adventures to find fulfillment. I'm glad we did this little trip. I really needed it to help clear my thoughts," said Thomas.

"At least you have a story to tell. How many people can say that they went through a night like we did?" asked Jorge.

"Not many," replied Thomas.

"It's your responsibility to enjoy life while you're young," said Victor. He was confused by Thomas' point as well.

"You're right," said Thomas.

"Imagine yourself at fifty years old, having accomplished everything that you ever wanted to accomplish professionally, but regretting all the other things that you missed out on; love, lust, people, conversations, friends, the sights of the world, the thrill. Sorry man, not for me," explained Victor.

Thomas knew that his friends had valid points about the importance of pleasure and experience. He paid attention to what Victor said about regret. The evening's events made him rethink how he'd been living for the past two years. "Maybe I just need a break from it all," he said to himself, although everyone else heard it.

The waitress returned to take everyone's order. Victor asked for a personal-sized sausage pizza. Chavez ordered the fondue. Jorge went with the paella and a side of refried frijoles. Thomas couldn't resist asking for the chicken curry.

Jorge felt his phone vibrate. He took it out of his pocket and saw that it was Helga once again. Jorge stared at the screen, flashing her name over and over again while the phone continued to vibrate.

"Why don't you pick up?" asked Thomas. He knew who was calling by the expressions on Jorge's face.

"Who is it?" asked Victor.

"The love of his life," answered Thomas.

"Eat shit, Flores," replied Jorge.

"Didn't she break up with you?" asked Thomas. I'm starting to see how crazy she is. Last night she called me to complain that I didn't call her mother on her birthday," answered Jorge.

"Why the fuck do you have to call her mother on her birthday?" asked Thomas.

"You have to remember that we were together for a long time, and her parents helped me out a lot after my parents divorced. Sometimes I think I miss them more than I miss Helga," said Jorge.

"You still miss Helga?" asked Chavez. Jorge's face said it all.

"Ahuevos, but I don't want to be with her. It's not healthy for either one of us. We were always fighting, and she had a way of making me go crazy over the dumbest things," he explained.

"My classmates told me that you once came to the school and started slamming on the classroom door because she didn't want to come out and talk to you. That's why they all think you're insane," said Thomas. Jorge was a proud representative of Guatemala's middle-class society.

"I don't give a fuck what those rich sons of bitches think. I spit on the wealthy class' opinion."

Victor laughed at Jorge's silliness. He found it hysterical every time he heard of a man losing control of his emotions over a woman. "So, why do you still talk to her?" he asked Jorge.

"Because we were together for more than five years, and I think I'm still trying to figure out my life without her. Like I said, I don't want to be with her anymore. I know that we are both better off without each other. She's already had two boyfriends since I left. She's the type of girl that always has to be with someone. And you know what, I don't want to be with her after she has been with someone else." His body slumped into the lawn chair; the topic wore him down physically and mentally. "Shit, one time she threatened to tell her parents that I hit her," he said.

Thomas always thought she was crazy. Jorge's story confirmed it. "She was pissed at me because I didn't want to be her nephew's Godfather. We got into an argument about it in the car, and she snapped," said Jorge. He looked at Thomas and continued, "You don't understand Thomas. Women in Guatemala are crazy. They want to be your mother more than your wife. I can honestly say that the relationship lasted as long as it did because of my parents' divorce. I knew I wasn't going to stay in Europe forever and that she was in Guatemala waiting for me when I got back." Jorge's hands were clenched from the tension that Helga caused him. "I was twenty years old and at the loneliest point of my life. She was there for me."

They were all very high and very full by the time the meal was over. The four friends stood outside the restaurant on the narrow road that went along San Pedro's entire mountain coast.

"That was a meal to remember," said Thomas.

"You want a cigarette?" asked Jorge as he pulled out a crushed-up pack of Marlboro Lights. Thomas graciously accepted.

Once again, they were without any real plan or direction. They stood in the middle of the road and idly wondered where to go next, left to the waterfall or right to the weed dealer's house. The day was getting hot, and nothing sounded more refreshing than a dip at the waterfall. Yet, the weed from San Pedro was so fresh and potent that buying it was a must.

Chavez volunteered to walk alone to buy the weed. "Last time I went to his house was when I came here with my cousin. It's just up the road, probably like a twenty-minute walk or something like that," he said. "Are you sure that you want to go by yourself?" asked Jorge.

"Si mon, it'll be fast. Take Thomas and Victor to the waterfall, and I'll be there soon with some fresh doobie," he said.

Chapter Eight
Chavez and the Revelation

The sun's heat had become unbearable. Thomas was thirsty. He stepped to the window of a small shop where a young female in white shorts was working. She was bent over, storing away some cans. Thomas couldn't help but stare into the deep crevice that marked her ass.

"Hola," he said gently, not to startle the girl. To Thomas' delight, her front was just as attractive as the back. She was a curvy girl with an angel's face. Thomas calculated her to be eighteen or nineteen years old. "I'm sorry. I didn't mean to startle you," he said politely.

"No, don't worry. It's just that I didn't expect anyone to come. How can I help you?" she responded in a friendly tone.

"Three Gallos, please," replied Thomas.

While the girl turned around to get the beers, Thomas motioned Jorge to join him at the window to show what he'd found. As soon as Jorge moved in to take a look, a second girl came out from a back room carrying a crate of empty soda bottles. She was just as, if not more, beautiful than the girl attending Thomas. She wore tight jean shorts and a yellow tank top that accentuated her firm breasts. Jorge's eyes instantly locked on her.

"How far is the waterfall from here?" he asked, starting a conversation.

"It's about two kilometers from here, but you're going to have to pass through a trail that takes you up the mountain,' said the girl in the yellow tank top who didn't mind Jorge trying to get a look down her shirt.

"And how is it? Is it any fun?" asked Jorge to keep the conversation going.

"The tourists seem to like it, but I prefer swimming in the lake because it's not as cold. I guess it depends on who you're with," said the girl in a playful tone. She smiled at Jorge, revealing her dimples. Jorge saw an opening and went for it.

"Bathing in that water sounds perfect right now. I'm so hot. Aren't you?" he asked while looking her directly in the eyes.

"I don't think it's going to be cold enough for you," she said. Jorge's smile grew more.

"Would you girls want to come with us?" asked Thomas. The girl in the white shorts immediately didn't like the idea and walked away. Her sister was less defensive. She popped the bottle caps and handed them the beers.

"How's it going to be convenient for us?" she asked.

"You'll have a day of pleasure," replied Thomas. The girl was charmed by his banter. She thought the handsome strangers were good-natured and harmless. Their presence offered a change in the lonely town of San Pedro.

The girl in the white shorts called her sister to the back of the store to discuss her concern. Thomas and Jorge could hear them arguing. The two friends drank their beers while leaning their backs against the window ledge. They watched Victor walk back and forth as he attempted to get a cell phone signal.

Jorge felt a poke on his shoulder. It was the girl in the yellow tank top.

"My sister doesn't want to go, so I'm just going to throw away the garbage, and then I can go with you." She went into the back again, leaving the shop completely unattended, which gave Jorge sufficient time to steal some emergency snacks.

They waited for fifteen minutes for the girl to return. Thomas and Victor grew impatient.

"If she doesn't come out in the next five minutes, we should start walking," said Thomas. He didn't want to waste the day.

"She's coming," said Jorge, who refused to lose any hope.

The girl in the yellow tank top came out with a look of disappointment on her face.

"Are you ready?" he asked.

She frowned and said, "My grandmother is on her way, and I have to be here when she comes."

"You're kidding, right?" asked Jorge.

"But as soon as she leaves, I'll meet up with you. It might take a little while, but I'll be there," she said.

Jorge, Victor, and Thomas parted ways with her and headed up the road.

Somewhere on the other side of town, Chavez was walking farther than he'd anticipated. It seemed that he was lost. "That shit wasn't so far from the docks, was it?" he asked himself. Chavez contemplated whether or not he should continue walking or turn around to catch up with his friends. An enormous responsibility had been placed in his hands, and he didn't want to disappoint them.

He heard a motor in the distance. It was a local taxi, a tuc-tuc. The teenage driver noticed Chavez standing on the side of the road with a confused look on his face. He pulled over, seizing the opportunity to make money.

"Do you know how to get to Alta Cruz?" asked Chavez. The boy paused and thought to himself, questioning Chavez's motives. He was well aware that Don Ronaldo, the biggest distributor of marijuana in the region, lived there.

"You still have about a kilometer to go. I can take you," said the boy after he assumed Chavez was a pothead by the way he was dressed, t-shirt, baggy cargo pants, and the afro. Chavez was perplexed at how bad his memory was. Then he remembered all the mushrooms he had taken with his cousin the last time he was there.

"How much will you charge me?" he asked the boy.

"Thirty quetzals," the boy replied. Chavez thought the price was steep, but he didn't want to walk in the unforgiving heat, and it seemed like the boy knew where he was going. "No, man, that's too much. Take me for twenty," he counter-offered. The street-smart kid gave another offer, "Twenty-five." Chavez was at the boy's mercy. He didn't know when he would see another tuc- tuc. "Alright, twenty-five, let's go."

The boy drove recklessly in his modified moped with an attached roof made of nothing more than a tarp and a few poles. Chavez held tightly to his seat as the tuc-tuc turned sharply up the narrow road. The young driver noticed Chavez staring at the remains of what was once a five-acre marijuana field. All that was left was a burnt marsh of organic material.

"That used to be a weed field," he told Chavez. "A week ago, the national police raided it and burned everything down," said the boy. Chavez imagined a giant cloud of weed smoke hovering over San Pedro and the entire area getting high for free.

"I would have gone to the fire and inhaled for as long as I could," said Chavez to the driver.

"Some kids were actually doing that. They just walked up as close as they could to the fire and took a seat on the dirt after the police left." Chavez wished he had been there.

"How much weed was it?" he asked.

"I think it was almost two acres," replied the boy.

After nearly a seven-minute ride, the tuc-tuc stopped in front of a stone path of stairs that led to someplace up the mountain. Chavez didn't find anything familiar about the area. According to his memory, the house was a small shanty, bordered by a broken-down fence where a couple of dogs roamed. It looked like the mushrooms from his previous visit were more potent than he had imagined.

"Here we are. How much did you want?" asked the boy. He didn't need Chavez to confirm that he was there to buy weed.

"Sixty," replied Chavez as he pulled out the cash that he had collected from Thomas and Jorge. He was impressed by the boy's instinct.

"Sounds good; he lives up those stairs. Wait here while I go and get it for you," said the young hustler. He turned off the ignition and disappeared into the thick vegetation, leaving Chavez to wait all alone with his thoughts.

Back on the other side of San Pedro, Jorge, Thomas, and Victor were walking up the untamed mountain path that led to the waterfall. The humidity was dreadful, dilating every pore on their skin as they released buckets of sweat with every step taken. The tunnel-like path seemed to ascend without any end in sight. It didn't take long before Thomas started to question his actions once again. He kept his opinion to himself and made a point not to complain.

They all huffed and puffed as the heat drained every ounce of their energy. Through it all, Victor maintained his sense of humor.

"If Chavez gets lost, he can just follow the river of ball sweat I'm leaving behind."

"There's not much left. We'll be able to see the waterfall after this drop coming up," said Jorge. The announcement did little to lift Thomas' spirit; each breath he took scraped his bare chest.

"This better be worth it, Palma," he said quietly. "We could have just smoked and took a dip in the lake. Instead, we're in this inferno with snakes, jaguars, and all types of shit." Shortly after that, they all heard something. There was thrashing in the distance.

"That's the water," said Jorge, who knew they'd arrived. The top of the path formed an opening to a majestic oasis concealed from the world.

The waterfall was as impressive as Jorge described. The water thrashed down from high above to create a pool that eventually emptied into the lake. The sun shone through the tree openings of the jungle, demonstrating a refractive glare that glistened above the water. But they weren't alone; it seemed as though someone else had the same idea.

Sara and Edgar drove to San Pedro after the rave. The sun was already out by the time they had left. Sara was sunbathing when she lifted her head and noticed the boys making their way down the mound. Jorge had texted his cousin before falling asleep, telling her where they were.

"Hi, boys!" she said while waving. Edgar was standing on a steep cliff with a rope swing and yelled out, "What are you girls doing here?" He took one last look at the water before swinging on the rope and executing a perfect cannonball.

Back on the other side of town, Chavez was peeing behind a tree. As it turned out, the driver didn't come back as soon as he said he would. Almost fifteen minutes had passed since the boy took his money and left. He started to wonder about his friends. It had been over an hour since they parted ways, and he was a little frustrated at the thought of them having fun while he was enduring the inconveniences of the mission.

With every passing minute, sweat continued to pour from his head. Chavez took off his hat to let his curly afro breathe for a second. He was tempted to leave, but he didn't want to lose the money he gave the kid. Chavez also knew that the boy would be back eventually for his tuc-tuc. After waiting a little longer, he finally came running down the walkway with a message for Chavez.

"He wants to talk to you," he told Chavez, who was only expecting a bag of weed and nothing else.

"Who? Me?" he asked.

"Yes, Don Ronaldo wants to talk to you. Let's go," urged the boy.

Chavez was confused. He'd already wasted the best portion of the day and wanted to get the hell out of there. Apart from that, he simply didn't want to wander into an unknown drug dealer's house because of the potential danger it could present. There were hundreds of kidnappings in Guatemala every year, and Chavez wasn't in the mood to become another statistic. There was a particular case that had recently occurred which was still fresh in the minds of many.

About a month earlier, the son of a Guatemalan diplomat was taken from the front steps of his home while waiting for the bus to school. The criminals jumped out of a car and viciously gunned down the innocent caretaker as she bravely tried to defend the child. They left a demand of two million quetzals for the safe return of the child. The family immediately reached out to every resource imaginable and miraculously came up with the money before the twenty-four-hour deadline. The child's safety was the primary concern of the police, so they followed the kidnappers' demands and delivered the money to a specified location near the department of Mixco. Unfortunately, the person who had organized the kidnapping had a deeply embedded disdain for the diplomat. The boy's parents waited all through the night to receive word of their son's location. The following morning, they received a phone call from a muffled voice that instructed them to walk to a nearby park where their son would be waiting. The parents were filled with anguish as they raced to the park on foot to the exact spot where the voice said their son was. They searched the area and couldn't find the boy until they arrived at the jungle gym and saw four human limbs hanging from a string. The little boy was brutally murdered, and the rest of the body was never discovered.

Chavez offered a prayer to God to keep him safe, put on his

hat, and followed the boy up the steps to see Don Ronaldo. To his surprise, the path led him to an open field with a soccer goal at the far end, a barbecue area with a fire grill made of bricks on the other, an empty horse stable, and a water well. They walked to the ranch house rather quickly, as though something urgent needed to be taken care of. It was a white, concrete home with a sturdy, straw roof.

They walked around to the far end of the house, where there was an old man wearing a white dress shirt, cargo shorts, and sandals. He was standing in front of an easel, painting an abstract acrylic of some sort.

"Señor, here he is," said the boy to the old man. For some reason, Chavez had a feeling that he was going to be interrogated. He stepped forward and extended his hand to Don Ronaldo. The man didn't take his hand. He stared near-sighted at Chavez with his inch-thick spectacles. Then he wiped his hands on the towel that hung around his neck and took off his glasses.

"Young wanderer, what are you doing here?" Chavez didn't know how to answer the question since he was baffled.

"The boy said you wanted to talk to me," he replied.

Don Ronaldo walked over to a picnic table and placed his brushes in a jar filled with Gamsol paint thinner, and then he sat down.

"I'll wait out front for you." said the tuc-tuc driver. He turned around and started to walk away.

Chavez called after him.

"Where's my money?"

The boy pointed at Don Ronaldo.

"He has it. Don't worry." He disappeared and left Chavez all alone with the old man.

"Why have you come here?" repeated Don Ronaldo.

"I wanted to buy some weed," responded Chavez. He didn't know what else to say.

"You are lost, and I know it," said Don Ronaldo. Chavez had no idea what the older man was talking about. "Take a seat," Don Ronaldo told him. Chavez listened. He figured the old man wasn't going to let him leave without saying what he needed to say, so he got comfortable. Chavez sat down, folded his hands, and looked directly at Don Ronaldo. Before speaking, the old man studied Chavez for a bit.

"When I was younger, a twenty-year-old baby, I thought that I would live forever. When my father died, he left my siblings and me each our own share of a large inheritance. I used my money to invest in a coffee business, which turned out to be a very profitable decision. It wasn't long before I became greedy for success. I partied like I was the greatest gift to this earth. With money, everyone wants to be your friend, and all the girls want to fuck you," said Don Ronaldo. "I didn't want to follow anyone's rules. So, I didn't." He picked up a weed bud and twirled it between his fingers. "I invested much of my profits in this little plant that was becoming so popular among kids like you; it was the sixties." He tossed the bud over to Chavez. "I would spend days shitting away whatever money I made on useless things like girls, clothes, and parties. I was a 'somebody' in a world of no-bodies. Do you understand? My mind became poisoned with greed, thinking that I was invincible within my little world of Retalhuleu." Don Ronaldo exhaled at the memories. "The life of a drug dealer can sometimes force a person to do things he normally wouldn't do. It's the heavy price that comes with the game."

The old man got up from his chair and unbuttoned his shirt, revealing two bullet wounds on the upper right side of his chest.

"This happened one night while I was returning home from the capital. I had just sold twenty pounds of marijuana to a man I had known for over fifteen years. As I was leaving the borders of the city, gunmen in a green Studebaker attacked me. I drove as fast as I could to escape, but their car was faster." Don Ronaldo pointed at his scars.

"They shot me three times, and my car flipped off the road."

"Did they come back?" asked Chavez.

"No. I think the accident drew too much attention, and they drove away. Some people found me and took me to a hospital," replied the old man. He shook his head, remembering the anger. "I was told that my associate of fifteen years, Rodolfo Sosa, ordered the hit. I looked for them for more than a year before I finally got my revenge.

Suddenly, Chavez was clinging to everything the man was saying.

"How did you kill them?" he asked. "One night, I received a tip that they were all at a nightclub, Rodolfo and his bodyguards. I went alone and waited for them to leave. I followed them to a late-night café where I walked in with a 9 mm and shot the bodyguards in the head."

Chavez couldn't believe what he was hearing. His body froze

with anticipation.

"And what happened to your associate?" he asked.

"He fell out of the chair and tried to get away from me. I let him get to the door to feel that it was locked. I wanted him to shit his pants and realize that he was about to be killed. He turned around to face me, and I shot him two times in the chest," replied Don Ronaldo. Chavez was speechless.

Don Ronaldo's voice changed. Sorrow crept in as he recollected his sins from the past. "I thought that revenge was going to make me feel better, but my conscience wouldn't allow it. There was blood on my hands. After that, I fell hard. I was lost, like you, my young friend." Chavez could only wonder how the old man came to such an accurate conclusion.

Don Ronaldo paused the story to see if any of the housemaids were nearby. He excused himself to see if any were around. He needed a drink to calm the constant shake of his hands.

Chavez noticed that Don Ronaldo's memories carried a heavy burden. Yet, through every layer of wrinkles, he saw the eyes of the regretful young man who vengefully murdered instead of forgiving.

"Eh, what's this girl's name?" he asked Chavez, who did not have a clue. "Eh, Lucrecia!" he yelled. "Bring me the Indita and two glasses!"

He returned his focus to Chavez, briefly pausing all movement as his brain remembered where it had left off. "My soul was overwhelmed by emptiness. The biggest problem was letting it all go. I continued to work independently with my suppliers, but the excitement that drove me deep into this business was gone. I wanted to run away from everyone and everything. It wasn't an easy thing to do when I would receive duffle bags of cash at least once a week. Until one day, it became clear to me that leaving it all was my only choice."

"What happened?" asked Chavez.

Don Ronaldo paused once again as his brain reverted to a horrid image from the past. "I saw my best friend, Severino, killed the same way that I had killed."

A housemaid walked over with a bottle of Indita, Guatemala's national moonshine. She set it on the table with two shot glasses. Don Ronaldo poured Chavez a drink before pouring himself one.

"We were both abducted in a drug deal and taken to a warehouse where we were met by Antonio Mendoza, a competitor of mine. Without hesitation, he put a pistol to Severino's head and shot him dead. I'd known him my entire life. Apparently, there were a lot of people mad at me for killing Rodolfo."

That's when Chavez asked the obvious question that anyone in his position would ask.

"And why didn't he kill you?"

Don Ronaldo was waiting for him to ask that.

Don Ronaldo raised his glass and said with a big smile, "Salud." Chavez raised his glass and said the same before drinking down the warm shot.

"Mendoza would have killed me, taken my supply, and left me for the maggots, except he wanted something."

"What?" Chavez asked.

"They wanted my entire supply. And they wanted me to work for them permanently because I was such a good producer of money. Poor Severino, he was just at the wrong place at the wrong time. He was killed to remind me that Mendoza wasn't fucking around."

With his hands crossed, Don Ronaldo momentarily sunk his head and stared at the wooden crevices on the table. "Now I had the blood of Severino on my hands. It was a burden that I couldn't handle." Chavez didn't know, but it was the first time Don Ronaldo spoke of his past in nearly fifty years. His soul could never relinquish the torment of his actions. It was his intention to let the pain and guilt kill him, slowly and unmercifully.

"So, what did you do?"

"I didn't ask any questions. I simply agreed to his demands, gave them what I had, and told them where my fields were. I was supposed to meet them the following day in Jutiapa to show them my methods. Instead, I left for Guadalajara and stayed there for thirty years."

The older adult stood up from the table and walked to a storage closet, where he grabbed an item from one of the shelves that were mounted on a wall. He walked back and placed down a fresh ounce of weed. Chavez was overwhelmed by the pungent, fruity odor. He took a big whiff. It created a scenario in his mind where he was joyfully bouncing inside the stuffed bag of crystallized buds.

"I'm sure you didn't expect to be talking to me about such a personal issue," said Don Ronaldo. He was prepared to confess something else that he knew could discredit his story, but it was something he felt he had to say. He became unusually nervous, puckering his lips together because he knew how bizarre things were about to get.

Sweat poured down his forehead and onto his glasses as he hesitated to get the words out of his mouth. "Young man, on two separate occasions, I experienced something that could only be described as divine intervention. Do you know what that is?" Chavez went to a catholic school for ten years and was well-educated on divine intervention.

"It's when God speaks directly to you in an unexpected way," replied Chavez.

The response told Don Ronaldo that Chavez was theologically prepared for what he had to say.

"In my situation, I believe that God spoke to me twice, in a dream and one day while I was working in the fields. Last winter, I was researching the different phenotype effects of temperature on male and female weed plants. I'd been out all morning, noting any obvious changes such as color, texture, and growth rate. At some point, I got hungry and started walking back to the house. I don't know why, but I became dizzy. For a brief moment, I lost my way in the pasture. I thought I was going to faint, and then I heard something."

"What did you hear?"

Don Ronaldo looked at Chavez sternly.

"I heard a loud voice in my head that said, *Believe in the Presence of Evil!* I was caught off guard. The voice was so powerful that I instantly repeated the words out loud, *Believe in the Presence of Evil!* Then a big gust of air forcefully shook the weed bushes. I didn't know what was happening, but as soon as I turned a corner, I saw a large black snake in the middle of the path standing itself straight up while staring me directly in the eyes like this." Don Ronaldo put his right arm on the table and raised his forearm in a way that emulated the snake's erect position. He brought his fingers together and pointed them at Chavez to form the snake's head. "I almost shit myself. I turned around, did the sign of the cross, and walked the other way reciting the Hail Mary until I got home."

Chavez wanted to grab the bag of weed and run. He didn't like the direction that Don Ronaldo had taken the conversation. Things were getting weird.

Don Ronaldo grabbed some fresh weed from his own personal stash and packed it in his homemade wooden pipe. He took the first hit and passed it over to Chavez, who graciously accepted. He thought it would ease his tension.

"I thought the incident had happened, and that was it. I didn't think that it would tie into my life in any other way until a couple of weeks ago. I had a dream." Don Ronaldo took a second hit from the pipe before passing it back to Chavez.

"In this dream, I found myself in the house where I grew up with my brothers and my mother. It must have been a birthday or some type of celebration because my entire family was there, smiling, drinking, and eating as we often did. At some point in the dream, I decided to climb the rooftop where I had spent many hours as a child thinking and dreaming. It was my favorite place in that busy house. At some point, I heard my mother call my name when the food was ready, so I went down to eat. As I was walking towards the balcony door, I heard a familiar voice yell my name. I got close to the edge of the roof and saw Severino hanging for his life. His head was injured and covered in blood. He kept asking, *WHY AREN'T YOU HELPING ME? WHY AREN'T YOU HELPING ME?* I balanced myself and reached down to grab him. As I started to pull him up, he looked me in the eyes and said, *'Give me guidance the next time I come around. You owe it to me.'* And then his face changed. It became a dark shadow with no eyes, mouth, or nose. The silhouette was that of a young man with curly hair wearing a baseball hat." Chavez had no idea how to respond to such a bizarre revelation.

Don Ramon continued, "I tried to pull him up, but I couldn't. The figure looked up at me one last time and said, 'Guide me when I'm lost, Ramon. Guide me when I'm lost.' Then he just looked down and let go."

Chavez was at a loss for words. He didn't know how to react to everything that he'd just heard. He found it hard to believe that the old man foresaw his visit through a revelation from God. Even after having witnessed a UFO the night before, he wasn't going to believe every improbable tale that was told to him suddenly. Still, he couldn't ignore the fact that the revelation was being presented to him at that particular moment when his faith was in such a vulnerable state. His mind was always open to the meaning of life and to the existence of a divine entity, but he wasn't necessarily prepared to accept everything that was coming his way.

"When the boy told me how you looked, I knew that you were the one. Whether it was Severino or some other force that appeared in my dream, I knew that the message was supposed to be given to someone else. I just didn't know who until today. I don't know the specifics of your life, but whatever it is that's stopping you from moving forward, you need to take it out of the equation," said Don Ronaldo as he slid the bag of weed across to Chavez with his hand.

Chavez left Don Ronaldo's ranch with a mess of thoughts swirling in his head. He didn't know how to process what he'd heard. Part of him wanted to find a significant meaning out of it, but it wasn't easy to give Don Ronaldo any proper credit. Chavez wondered if he was just an old and lonely stoner who was full of regret for the poor decisions that he made as a youth.

Back at the waterfall, Thomas, Victor, Jorge, Sara, and Edgar took advantage of their Saturday morning. The water's energy re-invigorated their souls as it washed away their sins from the previous evening. Sara and Jorge had a swimming race under the cold water from one end of the pool to the other. It was a game that they played as kids. Like always, Jorge swam underwater to show off while Sara performed a breaststroke as best as she could. The result never changed; Jorge always won.

Thomas walked along the slippery rocks that ran up the waterfall, cautiously stepping from rock to rock to get as close as he could to the cascade. He sunk his head into the thrashing water. The deafening power helped to soothe away the stress knots that accumulated along his neck and back muscles.

Without warning, Sara popped her head out of the water close to where Thomas was standing.

"Hey, give me your hand," she said to get his attention. It didn't take long for Thomas to recognize the potential of the situation. He and Sara always had an eye for one another, but Jorge was his friend, and he didn't think it would be fitting to make a move. He helped her up and took strong notice of her surprisingly athletic frame.

She walked close to the rushing water to drench her head. "Be careful. It's powerful," warned Thomas. She grabbed his arm and slowly stepped forward. The water poured down her body with great force. She stood firm and enjoyed every single drop.

Victor wasn't as eager as the others to get wet. He wanted to rest his body before letting the cold water shock his muscles. It was evident to the others that he was stalling, but they didn't know why. Jorge splashed some water on him.

"We're all here having a great time, and you're there fully clothed in this hot ass jungle," he said.

Lying down, Victor raised his head and said,

"In just a minute, I'm relaxing."

Victor was building up the courage to take off his clothes and walk into the water. He managed to go an hour without even taking off his shoes. Eventually, his patience and tolerance for the heat wore thin as the temperature continued to rise. After taking a deep breath, he stood up and removed his shoes and socks. Then, in a quick move that seemed as though it was meant to avoid attention, he took off his hat. Neither Thomas nor Jorge had ever seen him without a baseball hat, and now they knew why. Victor was thirty years old and almost entirely bald.

No one could believe it. Thomas and Jorge looked at one another and laughed silently without causing him any further embarrassment. Victor was tired of having to hide his baldness every time he went out in public. He realized that he didn't need to anymore because he was loved.

He took two steps into the water, held his breath, and dove in before resurfacing. His body jolted from the frigid water. "Oooofff," he said after catching his breath. Everyone else was glad to see him having a good time.

Jorge felt the urge to smoke a cigarette. He walked out of the water and looked through the pockets of his pants to find the mangled crush-proof pack.

"Thomas!" he yelled and held up the pack. "Do you want one?" Thomas didn't pay too much attention. Jorge noticed that he was flirting with Sara. Like many Latin American males, he had a strong and genuinely close relationship with his female cousin; but he wasn't jealous. Jorge was too free of a spirit to let something so insignificant bother him. Also, he trusted Thomas. Jorge didn't say anything and let the two explore each other in peace.

Lying down along the water's edge and soaking up the sun that seeped in between the tree branches, Jorge noticed a thin figure walking down a path on the other side of the waterfall. It was the girl with the yellow tank top. She opted to take the easier route to the waterfall, the same one that Edgar and Sara took, instead of marching through the mountains.

"Why don't you come over here!" he said to her.

She smiled back.

"I'll be right there!" she called.

The girl took off her shorts and top to expose her bikini. Jorge held his head up to admire the view.

The girl carefully stepped down the path and stood on a rock next to the water's edge. She took one last look at the crystal depth before diving in head first. She swam under the cold water to the other side where Jorge was waiting. She stood up and walked towards him. Jorge felt he was being seduced. He couldn't take his eyes off her body, which was dripping wet from head to toe.

"My grandmother can be a tyrant sometimes. I had to wait until she left before coming over," she said.

"It's okay. I'm glad you came," said Jorge with a charming smile on his face. "What's your name? I can't remember if you told me?" he asked.

"If you give me some of your beer, I'll tell you," she replied. It seemed to Jorge that the girl was looking for a good time.

"Absolutely, here you go," said Jorge as he passed her his liter of beer. The girl chugged the remaining third like a seasoned drinker. Jorge was impressed.

"My name is Rosario. Do you have another cigarette?" It was like she didn't want to waste a single second of her freedom. Jorge grabbed the pack from out of his pants and handed her one. She put it in her mouth, and he lit it for her.

Thomas and Sara continued to enjoy one another's company. The fact that they were both American dental students in Guatemala always gave them something to talk about. He felt that she could relate to his stress. Sara was originally born in Guatemala and had spent a good portion of her childhood living there. She moved to Tampa with her mother after her parents divorced. Spanish was her primary language, and she didn't have much difficulty understanding her lectures. Like Thomas, she was facing an unfamiliar collegiate system that lacked the necessary educational resources given in the United States.

"How's it going in anatomy?" he asked her as they sat in a tiny pool formed by boulders.

"Horrible! Thomas, it's going so bad for me, and I don't know what to do. I'm almost positive that I failed the semester and that I might get suspended," she said while shamefully laughing.

"What went wrong?" asked Thomas as though he didn't have his own theory developed as to why she failed. He knew Sara well enough to know that, like him, her party habits were partly to blame.

"I don't know. I study almost every day, but the professors tend to give us questions on the exam that no one knows anything about. And when we review the exams together with the professor, she tells us that it's our responsibility to conduct additional research on the main topics. It's like, it all seems very unfair to me like they want us to fail."

It was apparent to Thomas that she was frustrated like he was. "So, what are you going to do? Are you going to repeat the year or go back to Tampa?"

"What can I do? I have to get a job and work until the following semester begins. I don't think I'll go back to the States. I'm really enjoying the time with my father. What about you?" she asked.

"I don't know what the hell I'm supposed to do. If I'm even supposed to be here anymore," replied Thomas. Sara thought that Thomas was crazy for trying to study dentistry in Guatemala, but she didn't want him to quit.

"It's hard to live here, I know; but you can't abandon school. Isn't that the reason you came here in the first place?" she asked.

"Yeah, but that was two years ago before I even knew how to wipe my own ass." Sara laughed at Thomas' honesty.

"What are you saying? You don't want to try to be a dentist anymore? You want to give up everything that's waiting for you back home?" Sara referred to the opportunity of owning his father's dental practices.

"It's just that I don't know if I'm in control of my own destiny anymore," said Thomas. "If I had things my way, I would've stayed in the U.S. and gone to dental school there. I studied my ass off all throughout college and prepared myself for my entrance exam. I moved to North Carolina to raise my GPA and work as a research assistant. And in the end, all of my efforts were for nothing. Life didn't give a shit about my plan. I thought I was making the right decision by coming here. But the same thing happened. I studied my ass off, and it just wasn't good enough," said Thomas.

"Maybe you just have to study a little more," said Sara. Thomas was surprised to hear her say that. He thought it was something that he should be telling her.

"That's impossible. I understand all the material and review it over and over again. I even record the lectures so that I can go back home and listen for anything I might have missed. To be honest with you, I'm starting to feel that no matter how hard I try to go down this path, God keeps redirecting me down another path," confessed Thomas.

Sara was caught off guard by his response but admired his honesty.

"Something else like what?" she asked.

"That's something I need to figure out," said Thomas.

"It seems like you put it all on the line when you came here. If you're not happy with what you've been doing, then maybe you need to stop overthinking it and make a choice," advised Sara.

"Do you think it's that easy?" he asked. Thomas wanted her to say yes.

"I don't know, Thomas. I can't imagine that it will be easy to start over at your age. You need to make up your mind before it's too late. You don't want to live the rest of your life stuck doing something you don't love," replied Sara.

She dipped her head under the water and grabbed Thomas's hand to keep from slipping. Thomas liked the way her baby soft skin felt.

"Personally," she said as she lifted her head, "I think God's been revealing an answer to you for a while. You need to listen to whoever or whatever it is that's been guiding you this whole time and do what feels right." Thomas appreciated her response.

"You know, for a struggling dental student, you're pretty smart," he said before dipping his head underwater.

On dry land, Jorge and Rosario stepped away for a bit of privacy. Thomas and Sara saw them grab some items and walk into the trees.

"Where do you think they're going?" asked Sara. He knew that Jorge was probably going somewhere to have sex.

"They're probably just going for a walk, you know, to talk," he said to avoid unnecessary drama.

Thomas carefully stepped away from the falls and towards the spot where Jorge left his pants. He found the weed case in the pocket. There was a minimal amount left. Knowing that Chavez was purchasing more, he used what was left to roll a joint.

Minutes later, Thomas and Sara were sitting side-by-side,

passing the joint to one another, letting the THC saturate their blood. Halfway through the joint, they both settled into a personal drift of thought. They both gazed at the greenery, at the sky and at everything else that surrounded them. Their brains were fixated on the relaxing pulse that was swarming through their bodies. The capacity to think and express their words in a meaningful way had become dormant, leaving Thomas and Sara to enjoy the beauty of the moment together.

Thomas knew that there was no other place on the planet where he was supposed to be. Under that waterfall, he was gaining the courage to start his life over. Thomas understood that he was going to have to find his calling all alone, fearlessly, and without regret. He felt the urge to mark his epiphany with an act of bravery. He saw a thirty-foot rope hanging from a small cliff on the mountain wall. It was much higher than the one Edgar used. He figured the rope was there because someone had already determined the area to be a safe jump point. "Hey, check this out," he said to Sara, who hadn't a clue of what he was thinking of doing.

Thomas swam to the wall and reached up to grab the rope. There was nowhere in the vicinity to stand. He placed his feet on the wall and gave the rope a few hard tugs to test if it could hold his weight. After determining that it was safe to climb, Thomas wrapped the rope twice around his right wrist and pulled himself out of the water. He relaxed his butt and kept his feet planted firmly on the wall. The position allowed him to shift the resistance of the climb onto his powerful arms and back.

Thomas began to ascend the wall with ease. Sara was impressed with his natural strength and very much turned on by his physical build. He alternated between hands, one pull after the other, flexing every muscle fiber until he reached the steep cliff.

"Oh shit," he said after realizing how high he'd ascended. The water thrashed down next to him with a deafening force as he built up the courage to jump. He closed his eyes and took a few deep breaths. He thought of everything that was weighing down his mind. He thought of the pain that he still held from his grandfather's passing. He thought of his guilt, sadness, loneliness, and fear of failure. He breathed in positive vibes and breathed out the negative. Once his mind felt free, Thomas opened his eyes, and he looked down once more into the bottomless pit of water.

"Let's do this!"

Victor was watching him the entire time and yelled encouragement from down below.

"Let's go, Thomas!"

Thomas jumped as far as he could, plunging more than thirty feet into the water. Sara was amazed by his unpredictable act. Victor and Edgar stood up to see if he was okay after going underwater. It was a forceful impact. Their concern was the crushing rocks at the bottom of the pool. Thomas was nowhere to be seen.

Unknown to his friends, Thomas could hold his breath for over two minutes. He swam underwater to a rocky area where he could stand and not be seen. He peaked his head to see if they were panicking. Instead, he realized that they were all in dangerous trouble.

There were two men with guns standing at the higher end of the waterfall. Victor, Sara, and Edgar were all in the water with their hands up, looking up at the armed criminals. Thomas didn't recognize either one of them; he thought they were just some local hooligans looking to steal some cell phones. One had tattoos on his entire torso, neck, and face. The other was shirtless and had tattoos on both arms.

Thomas crouched behind a large rock where he seemed to be out of everyone's sight. He noticed the two men yelling at Edgar about drugs. It was Smiley and one of his loyal followers, Massacre, of the 16th Street Mafia. "You found my bag at Devil's Factory, and I want it, you piece of shit!" shouted Smiley.

"I swear to you, I don't know what you're talking about!" replied Edgar. He was willing to risk everyone's life for a few ounces of cocaine.

Thomas noticed how scared Sara was. He didn't know what to do. His instinct was telling him to play the hero and distract the thugs while his friends ran away to safety. He hesitated for fear that his actions would lead to someone's death or his own. Smiley had the advantage of having a higher view, and Thomas didn't know precisely how far he could move before becoming an easy target.

Smiley pointed his gun at Edgar while his accomplice covered Victor and Sara. There was nowhere for them to run. Victor slowly stepped in front of Sara to protect her. The mad leader of the 16th Street Mafia made it known to everyone that his patience had worn thin. "You had me searching all over this fucking place for you. I want what you took, and I want it now," said Smiley.

The other gangster could care less about retrieving the cocaine.

"Let's just kill them and forget about the other shit. He's not going to tell us, and no one's around. We can leave the bodies here to rot."

Smiley assessed the situation. He wanted to satisfy his thirst for blood too. Still, he had suppliers who were expecting their full cut. He needed the drugs for the money it was worth.

"Massacre, go down and tie them up. If he doesn't say anything, we'll kill the girl first. And if he doesn't say anything after that, we'll kill the other motherfucker. And if he still keeps his mouth shut, we'll torture him," said Smiley.

"Orale, boss," said Massacre with a devilish stare in his eyes.

The shirtless gangster with the tattooed chest and arms carefully walked down the path that led to the water. Smiley kept his gun pointed at Edgar, Victor, and Sara, who were all worried and scared that they were going to die. Massacre was getting close to Thomas, who desperately looked around for something that he could use as a weapon. He found a rock that fit perfectly in his hand and then stepped back to avoid being seen. Massacre made it to the water's edge, took off his shoes, and tucked his gun into his pants. Thomas knew he had to act, or else they would all die. He pumped himself up with three full breaths in succession and made his move.

Thomas got right behind Massacre and smashed the gangster over the head with the rock. Massacre's body fell into the water, putting him in danger of drowning. Smiley was caught off guard by the unexpected counter-attack. He aimed at Thomas and fired four rounds from the 9mm. Thomas pulled back behind the rock and yelled, "Run!" to Edgar, Victor, and Sara.

Victor grabbed Sara's hand, and they bolted the opposite way into the jungle. Smiley shot twice at them, but his aim wasn't good, and he missed. Smiley was a street thug, not a soldier. He looked back to find Thomas, but he wasn't anywhere to be seen. He was somewhere under the water. Smiley quickly ran down to see if Massacre was alive. He found him by the rocks trying to regain his composure. There was a significant amount of blood seeping from the back of his head and down his neck.

Smiley grabbed the groggy accomplice by the arm to help him stand on his feet. It didn't take long for him to grow impatient.

"Let's go, you asshole. They're getting away," he said while pulling him urgently by the arm.

Thomas emerged from the water and ran as fast as he could to the protection of the jungle. Smiley was caught off guard once again. He fired off four shots. Every bullet missed, and Thomas was able to make it safely into the jungle. Victor, Sara, and Edgar were waiting for him with his clothes and shoes.

Victor and Thomas got dressed, while Edgar and Sara had no other choice but to wear their wet swimsuits. They heard the gangsters walking through the water and closer toward them, so they ran down the mountain path as fast as they could. It didn't take long to find Jorge. He was having sex in the dirt with Rosario. They were both completely naked, having sex doggy style. No one stopped to wait for them or explain in detail why they were running. Sara just dropped Jorge's clothes and kept moving.

"They're following us with guns. Hurry!" yelled Thomas.

With little hesitation, Jorge detached himself from Rosario, got dressed, and ran in the same direction that his friends were running. Rosario followed, wearing only a bikini, with her palms, forearms, knees, shins, and feet stained with jungle mulch.

Smiley wasn't far behind. He was determined to kill Edgar and his friends before they could catch a water taxi back to Panajachel.

Massacre lagged behind, stumbling from time to time. He huffed and puffed as his body grew weaker and weaker. He was losing a significant amount of blood from the gash in the back of his head. He didn't know it, but he was feeling the effects of a concussion.

Once they all reached San Pedro's main road, Rosario decided not to get any more involved than she already was. She ran behind her grandmother's store without saying goodbye. Jorge didn't even notice. He and his friends were focused on leaving San Pedro. Their bodies were pumped with adrenaline from the fear of death.

Not too far away, on the same road, Chavez was walking back from Don Ronaldo's house. He was hoping to see that his friends didn't leave without him and that there was still time to cool off at the waterfall. The walk back didn't seem as long as the journey it took to get to Don Ronaldo's house. Chavez felt different, as though some sort of weight had been lifted off his shoulders. He was walking at a lighter pace. Perhaps it was all the alcohol and weed, but Chavez was feeling a blessed euphoria of clarity.

Somewhere by the docks, little Leopoldo and little Gloria were showing a lesbian couple from Montreal a dual-juggling act. The two tourists were charmed by the performance of the little native children, but they didn't want to waste the day standing by the boats. They continued down the road without leaving a tip. Still, Leopoldo was insistent on offering them his services. "Do you need someone to show you around? I can take you to the market or to a restaurant if you're hungry." Gloria, as always, followed behind her older brother without ever saying a word.

Leopoldo went to one of the cafes and found a tuc-tuc driver who was enjoying a frijole sandwich while watching highlights from the Barcelona game. When the driver heard that two ladies needed a ride, he scarfed down the remaining half and went to offer his services. The two women were glad that they were approached by the driver. They had no idea that Leopoldo was the one who set up the accommodation and left without offering a tip.

Not too long after finishing a sketch of his sister on the sidewalk, Leopoldo saw Jorge and the others running back to the dock. He sensed the urgency and ran back to the boat to inform the driver. "The muchachos from this morning are coming back!"

Nearing the dock, Jorge noticed a thin man with a big curly afro strutting down the road. As they turned the last corner, Jorge stopped and yelled, "Chavez, hurry up! They want to kill us!"

Chavez didn't immediately take Jorge seriously.

"Eat shit, Palma! Here's your fucking weed! I hope you shove it up your ass!"

He was oblivious to what was happening. He didn't expect to see Sara and Edgar running back to the boat with the others. "Where's everyone going?" he said while holding up the bag of weed. Then he saw two men in the far distance running after his friends. That's when Chavez realized that he needed to get to the boat as fast as he could.

Thomas was the first to arrive at the boat; the others followed right behind him. Thanks to Leopoldo, the taxi driver had the engine running.

"There are two criminals running after us. Get out of here, or we're all dead!" said Thomas to the driver. Without hesitation, the man untied the noose and pushed off the dock.

Chavez turned the corner as the boat was pulling away. His

friends kept yelling at him to run faster. Smiley turned the corner as well with his gun cocked and loaded. He took aim at Chavez and started to fire. Every- one but Jorge ducked. He wanted to make sure that his friend would make it in safely. Sara pulled Gloria and Leopoldo down and covered them with her own body.

With a giant leap, Chavez threw his body into the boat. Smiley and Massacre emptied their clips in a last desperate attempt. The driver immediately pulled back the throttle and sped away from the pueblo of San Pedro. Smiley and Massacre stood breathless at the edge of the dock as they saw the boat ride away.

"Where do you think they're going?" asked Massacre.

"To Pana, let's go!" urged Smiley. They turned around and went back to their car.

Chapter Nine
The Beast Rides

After a half hour, the water taxi arrived at Panajachel. The driver was happy to see his unwanted customers go. He was worried that his participation in the event would compromise his peaceful life on the water. The passengers exited the boat one after the other. Thomas made sure to compensate the driver for his troubles.

"Look, I don't know why you waited, but thanks," he said before giving the man a tip of two hundred quetzals.

"Thank you," said the driver, who was grateful for the tip. Lastly, Thomas turned to Leopoldo and Gloria and gave them each one hundred quetzals.

"Thank you for everything, my friends," he said to them. The children took their earnings and went off to find something to eat.

There was a nervous tension in the air. Everyone felt it on the walk back to the car, especially Sara. She was still getting over the gunshots and the fact that there was someone trying to kill them.

"Thomas, please get us home quick," she said as they arrived at Panajachel's main road. Sara wasn't crying, but she was at a breaking point.

"Don't worry, I'll get us all home," he assured her.

They got to the car. Thomas popped open the trunk to find clothes for Sara and Edgar. Luckily for Sara, he found an extra pair of cargo pants and sneakers that an old girlfriend left behind after a weekend at the beach. He found a clean T-shirt in his back seat and gave it to her as well.

Thomas also found something for Edgar to wear, but he wasn't very interested in taking the clothes. Edgar had already decided that he wasn't leaving, not without the cocaine.

"Hey Jorge, I don't think that I'm going with you guys," he said.

"Why not?" replied Jorge. He couldn't think of any logical reason that Edgar would want to stay in Panajachel.

"I want to go back and get my car. That piece of shit probably left already, and I don't want anyone else to come along and steal it," answered Edgar.

"Forget about that shit. If Smiley sees you, he's going to put two bullets in your head without hesitation. Just leave the car there and come with us," said Thomas, out of disbelief.

Edgar didn't know what else to say. He was fixed on going back.

Jorge knew there was something more to the situation. "What the fuck do you have in that car?" he asked. The question put Edgar on the spot. Everyone's eyes were locked on him. He struggled to come up with a lie.

"What was in the fucking car, Edgar?" asked Jorge once again.

"I'm going back because I have his drugs in my car. It's taped underneath the trunk," replied Edgar.

No one could believe their ears. It was Edgar's fault that they became involved, and now their lives were in danger. He was a self-absorbed nomad who only looked out for his own interest. He was a survivor.

"I don't think he's going to stand around my car, waiting for me to come," he said to try and downplay the seriousness of the situation.

"No, you piece of shit, he's going to be waiting for us once we get back on the highway!" said Jorge.

"You should have just fucking told him where the drugs were, and we wouldn't be in this shit!" yelled Thomas.

Edgar didn't like being yelled at. He lashed out at the others like a man sick with greed.

"If you didn't want to get involved, then you should've stayed where you were and not hit the other guy with a rock! We didn't know if they were going to kill us or not," said Edgar. That was a blatant lie, and everyone knew it.

"I did it because they were going to kill you, you piece of shit, you, Sara, and Victor!" said Thomas.

Edgar threw a punch that connected with Thomas' mouth. Thomas barely flinched and threw a right cross to Edgar's eye. The punch leveled Edgar to the floor, nearly knocking him out. Victor interfered and held Thomas back from doing any further damage. It wasn't Thomas' intention to do so. Edgar slowly regained his composure and got back on his feet. He looked at everyone staring at him, still defiant.

"I'm going to get my money." He turned around and walked back to the water. The empowering temptation of money infected his mind the second he found the package. Only death could take it away from his possession. Everyone else stepped into the Lancer and closed their doors.

Thomas turned on the ignition, bringing his monster to life. Before backing out, he had a private moment in the car. He placed both of his hands on the steering wheel and whispered to the vehicle,

"Get us home safe, my friend."

Thomas didn't know it, but the car he boosted was about to be put to the ultimate test. He thought car racing was just a hobby to pass the lonely time in Guatemala, but it all had a greater purpose.

They drove up the winding road towards the main highway that brought them to Panajachel. Everyone was quiet. They were worried that Smiley was going to be waiting for them once they got to the highway. Victor, being the oldest of the group, understood the power of calmness and held his composure. He wasn't going to worry about something that had not yet happened. Thomas was also worried, but he was wearing his game face. He was focused on the task at hand to get his friends home. He felt confident that his car was built for the job. It had a front protecting bar, new shocks, and Kevlar bulletproof laminates on the windows.

Sara became more scared the closer they got to the highway. Jorge looked back to check on her and noticed that her eyes started to water. He tried to calm her down by toning down the seriousness of the situation. "Don't overthink it, Sara; nothing is going to happen," he said as Chavez put his arm around her neck. "Ahuevos Sara, once we get on the highway, I'll roll a joint to help you calm down. Jorge is right. Nothing is going to happen."

They drove past a sign **[Carretera 30 metros]**. Thomas wanted to give his friends a warning before reaching the highway.

So, he stopped the car on the side of the road.

"Why did you stop?" asked Jorge. Thomas didn't reply. He held a focused look on his face as he stared at the highway in front. There was a whirlwind of thoughts and emotions gathering in his head. Thomas was harnessing his fears just in case he found himself in a situation where there wasn't time to think. He was in a frozen state of mind; his instinct would now be his greatest companion.

Thomas took a deep breath, put the car in neutral, and. stepped on the accelerator. The tires peeled off the road and sent smoke flying into the air. Thomas put the car in first gear, then in second gear, and sent the vehicle into a turbo-propelled launch. He drifted the car onto the highway with his right hand on the emergency brake and his left hand on the wheel. The exhaust system reached a deafening frequency as the RPMs reached the odometer's red line. Everyone else held on to whatever they could grab as he sped through the winding highway. There was no time to slow down.

They'd been on the highway for a half hour without any sign of Smiley. The tension had toned down. The farther they drove, the less anyone worried that Smiley would show up. Even Sara had calmed down. She'd fallen asleep while resting her head on Chavez's shoulder. She hoped that the next time her eyes opened, everything would be fine, and they would be pulling up in front of her house. Very little was being said among the others. They were exhausted from the enormous overload of events that happened.

Victor was glad that he was going home to Kayla. He hadn't been his usual self all morning. Instead, thoughts of her were trapped in his mind. After having been shot at by a cold-blooded murderer, the only thing that he could think of was being underneath the covers with her where it was safe.

They approached a green sign along the highway **[GUATEMALA 50 KM]**. It was a relief for everyone to see. They all felt the danger was over and that they would soon be home.

"Hey Thomas, can you lend me a phone call? I have to call my father and let him know we're almost home. If not, he'll get pissed," said Jorge.

Jorge called his father. "I'm with Sara. We're coming home from Pana. We'll be home in an hour," he told him. His responsibility was complete, and he passed the phone to Chavez. He knew his parents were already pissed, so he called his sister, Claudia, instead.

"Hello? Geoffrey? Where the fuck are you?" she whispered.

Chavez could hear his parents arguing in the background.

"I was in Pana, but don't tell them that. Tell them that I slept over at Jorge's house, and we're going to the movies, and I'll be home after that," he said.

Claudia walked out the front door of her house to warn Chavez.

"The old man is saying that he's going to make you take a drug test. Last night, Mom went through your room and found your pipe."

Chavez could hear his father asking Claudia if it was him on the phone.

"Hurry up," she whispered before hanging up the phone.

To celebrate the end of their adventure, Jorge rolled a joint of Don Ramon's Oaxaca. He and Thomas both took a couple of hits before passing the joint to Chavez. Then, something strange happened. It seemed as though, after everything that had happened, the entire journey through the highlands culminated in one single moment. Chavez refused the joint. Normally, Jorge would have made light of the uncharacteristic gesture, but he saw a certain level of sincerity in Chavez that wouldn't allow him to disrespect his oldest friend.

Victor also refused the joint. He was busy admiring the vastness of the countryside. Plus, he wasn't feeling as vulnerable anymore. The mini-getaway made him come to grips with his own flaws. All he wanted to do was get back to normalcy and figure out how to keep his girlfriend happy.

The smoke filled the car as everyone admired the organic terrain that sat freely under the solid blue sky. Victor pointed out the window and towards the mountains.

"This is what I had always thought China looked like," he said to Chavez.

"But don't you have similar landscapes in Peru?" asked Chavez.

"Kind of; there's a lot more vegetation here. And the volcanoes are scattered everywhere. I'm from Trujillo, the beach," replied Victor.

"Ahuevos," agreed Chavez.

"Jorge!" Sara screamed. She was the first to see Smiley and Massacre pull up next to the Lancer. They were in a midnight blue Subaru WRX.

They were followed the entire way from Panajachel. Smiley had kept a safe distance in order to ambush them close to the capital, where he could make a clean getaway. His obsession had reached its boiling point, and he wanted nothing more than to kill Edgar and his friends. All Thomas could do was drive as fast as he could and hope to outmaneuver the pursuing vehicle. He knew that it was his responsibility to get his friends home safely. There was no more room left for hesitation in his life, Massacre, who was still bleeding from the back of his head, cocked back the barrel of his gun.

"Aim for the tires," said Smiley. The goon did as he was told. He leaned his body outside the window and took fire at the Lancer''s tires. The first bullet missed its target and hit the rear bumper.

"They're shooting at us!" yelled Jorge.

Thomas looked at the side mirror and saw that Massacre was taking the second aim. "Everyone, cover your head and get down!" he shouted. He cut off a fruit truck to get out of the way. Massacre fired the weapon and managed to hit the left taillight.

"Let's go, you worthless piece of shit! Either you shoot the tires, or I'm going to shoot you!" threatened Smiley. Massacre wasn't going to take his word lightly.

Smiley got the Impreza closer to the Lancer to give Massacre a better shot.

"Dead! Do you understand? I want them dead," he yelled.

Thomas tried speeding away, but he wasn't able to dodge the next bullet. Massacre hit the rear driver-side window. The bullet was stopped by the bulletproof laminate that was installed. If another bullet hit the same window, it would penetrate.

The road narrowed. The pursuit was now happening on a single-lane, two-way road. Thomas' palms were slippery with sweat as he gripped the wheel to drive with precision. He remained focused on the next move, trying to gain distance from Smiley. It wasn't an easy task because Smiley's car delivered higher performance.

The oncoming traffic made it impossible for Smiley to maneuver his car next to Thomas. He tried, but a small hatchback zoomed the other way. On the second attempt, he was approached by a speeding Seat, causing him to immediately swerve back into his lane. Thomas wasn't able to gain much ground either. Up ahead, he spotted an overcrowded bus that was transporting workers from Quetzaltenango to the capital. He wanted to cut it off at the right moment in order to prevent Smiley from mimicking the same move. No one else in the car was aware of his dangerous plan.

Smiley found a small window and passed the car in front of him to pull up behind the Lancer. He had Thomas right where he wanted. If he couldn't run the Lancer off the mountain, he was still in a good position to shoot out the back window.

"Now you can't fuck up. Shoot these mother fuckers!" said Smiley.

Massacre leaned his body out of the window and locked his aim on the back of the Lancer. Thomas looked at his side mirror and saw the man's arm steadily pointing the gun at his car. Either he made his move to get away, or Massacre would hit his mark.

Thomas yelled out to his friends, "Everyone leans to the left!"

"What the fuck are you going to do?" yelled Jorge.

Before he could get an answer, Thomas sped past the bus, drifting the vehicle against the mountains' edge. He cut dangerously in front of the bus at full speed, using all his focus to maintain the car's control. An inch more, and he wouldn't have made it. The bus driver cursed at him and repeatedly honked the horn while flashing the high beams.

Smiley wasn't going to let the car get away that easily. Massacre held on to the door handle and made the sign of the cross. Smiley put the car into fifth gear and sped in front of the bus. Once again, the bus riders looked on as the Impreza veered close to the edge of the mountain. Thomas was able to gain a safe distance, but he knew that it would only be temporary.

Jorge turned around to see if Sara was okay. Chavez had his arms covering her head to protect her from the danger.

"Don't worry, Sara. We'll be home soon," said Jorge. It was hard for him to fully believe what he'd just said, especially after he looked up and saw the Impreza heading toward them again.

The chase continued through the steep curves and winding roads. Massacre was unable to get a clear shot until the road finally straightened out. He took aim and hit the rear windshield twice, shattering it completely. Shards of glass flew everywhere inside the car.

Neither Massacre nor Smiley was content with shooting out the windows. They wanted blood.

"Pull up next to the passenger window. I'm going to get these fuckers, once and for all," said Massacre. He moved his body out the window, sat on the door, and used the roof to rest the gun for better aim.

Thomas felt that Massacre was in a vulnerable position. In order to take advantage of the situation, he would need to make a risky move. Massacre gripped the 9mm with both hands and aimed steadily at Jorge's window. He let off one shot to break the bulletproof laminate. Just as Massacre took aim for a second shot, Thomas sped up and slammed his car against the Subaru. Massacre flew off the car to his demise.

"Ignacio!" yelled Smiley. He tried to catch him, but it was too late. Massacre hit the road head first, crushing his skull before rolling to a lifeless halt.

Smiley's fury erupted. He leaned back and reached for a gun behind the passenger seat. It was one of many that were hidden within the cars' compartments. It was no longer a mission about retaining drugs. He became a man possessed with killing anyone who was in the Lancer. His sole purpose was to spill their blood.

Jorge saw a sign along the highway that brought hope. It was for the exit to Guatemala City, which was only two kilometers away.

"The exit's coming!" yelled Jorge. He could barely hear his own voice. His ears were ringing from the sound of the gunshots.

"To the left or to the right?" asked Thomas.

"To the right!" yelled Jorge.

Once off the exit, they could lose Smiley within the narrow streets that lay in between the busy avenues, Smiley knew it was their plan, so he acted to prevent it. He caught up and immediately slammed Thomas' car.

"You mother fucker!" screamed Thomas.

He veered to the left and slammed on the brakes, letting the Subaru move ahead. When his position was right, Thomas used the leverage to slam the side of Smiley's car. It skid off the road, losing control and nearly crashing into a tree. Unfortunately, Thomas' move made him miss the exit to the capital. They were now heading towards the Pacific coast.

"You just passed the exit," said Jorge.

"Where can we go?" asked Thomas.

"I'm trying to think," replied Jorge.

Thomas didn't have time to wait for Jorge to think. He needed an answer because Smiley was catching up.

"Just tell me how to lose this guy. I'm running out of ideas," said Thomas with urgency.

The Impreza was too fast to escape. Smiley was holding the wheel with his left hand and pointing the gun in a cross position with his right hand. Thomas turned his head and looked his enemy in the eyes for the first time. His body froze when he saw the gun pointing at his head. Time stopped, and everything went silent. The only thing he could focus on was Smiley's face; the ugly snarl, his gold grill, the tattoos that covered every inch of his brown skin, and his bald head. Thomas thought that he was about to die. He thought that Smiley finally had his shot.

Without warning, Smiley slammed into a white truck at a speed of ninety miles per hour. The impact killed him instantly. His car flew through the air and landed somewhere along the mountainside. Through the grace of God, the Lancer passed the collision and drove away with everyone unharmed.

Victor reached from the back seat and kissed the back of Thomas' head.

Thank you for not killing us," he said.

"Oh shit! I can't believe that just happened. Is everyone okay? Sara, are you okay?" asked Jorge.

"Yes, I'm fine," she replied as she brushed the broken glass from her clothes.

"Thomas, your car..." she said out of concern.

"It's alright. I'm just glad we're alive," he said.

"We should hide out in a pueblo. There are going to be a lot of cops driving around," said Jorge. Thomas made a sharp turn down a road that went through a sugar cane field. He had no clue where it led, but he went anyway. Maybe it was a direct result of the adrenaline going through their bodies or the excitement in the car, but nobody read the large street sign that said **[Cuidado: Volcan Activo].**

Chapter Ten
Surpassing Your Fears

Mercedes walked out of her private bathroom, drying her wet hair with a towel. There was an emergency news update on the television that caught her attention. She saw a male journalist standing in Antigua's central park with Volcan Pacaya in the background. Geologists were predicting a massive explosion. There were large amounts of smoke being expelled from its crater. The site created a sense of worry within her abdomen. All she could think of was Thomas and whether or not he was somewhere safe.

"Thomas, where are you?" she whispered to herself. She listened carefully to the details of the event given by the journalist.

...No se sabe el impacto que va tener la erupción, pero todos aqui se estén preparando para lo que sucede. Los departamentos de Escuintla, Cuilapa, Fraijanes, Sacatepe- quez, y Guatemala estardn en un estado de alerto rojo por el resto del dia. Residentes de Antigua estan haciendo lo que pueden para asegurar que sus pertenencias y sus familias estén fuera de peligro. Volcdn Pacaya queda a unos veinte ycuatro kilémetros de aqui y los efectos de la erupción definitivamente trae mucho miedo y inseguridad a residentes yturistas.

Commotion saturated the streets of Antigua. A large crowd in front of the central cathedral had actually gathered for a better view of the explosion. Others were leaving their homes behind and evacuating the city. All the stores were closed, and tourists were being told to remain indoors until it was deemed safe by the police to do otherwise. Five hundred years had passed since the last time Antigua was destroyed by a volcanic eruption; the possibility of it happening again was certainly possible.

Mercedes grabbed her phone from the nightstand and called Thomas at his apartment to see if he was home. The phone rang six times before she hung up. The fact that Thomas didn't answer made her more nervous. She tucked her bottom lip under her top teeth and thought of his whereabouts before attempting to reach him on his cell phone. The call went straight to his voicemail.

She hung up and tried a second time. Again, he didn't answer. A knot in Mercedes' stomach felt unbearably tight. She was worried that her beloved Thomas was in danger and unaware of it. The reporter called it a 'once in a lifetime event' Mercedes knew that Thomas was old enough to take care of himself, but Guatemala was, at all moments, a dangerous and unpredictable place. If there was one thing she knew for sure, it was that Thomas, wherever he was, wasn't abiding by anyone's rules other than his own.

Mercedes tried a few more times to get a hold of Thomas. Each attempt was unsuccessful. She sent him a text message [Hi! Where are you?]. She waited to receive a response, but he didn't reply.

"...queremos que todos hagan lo necesario en previsión de los temblores."

The news was forecasting heavy tremors, which made the roads dangerously unstable. She continued to listen for breaking news updates with her cell phone tightly gripped in her hand.

Somewhere outside the capital, the heavily damaged Lancer was driving up a steep road to an unknown destination. Jorge and Chavez were trying to figure out exactly where they were. The area was familiar to both, but the greenery was so dense that it made it difficult to determine where they were.

From the high elevation, the view was incredible. The horizon was marked by numerous volcanoes and mountains that traveled as far as the eye could see. "Where are we? Do I keep driving?" asked Thomas.

"For now, it's the only choice. I don't think you want to attempt a three-point turn on this road," suggested Jorge. Thomas looked over his left shoulder and noted Jorge's point. There was nowhere to go but up.

Eventually, they came to a fork in the road. Thomas stopped the car, and everyone looked around for anything that indicated their location. Victor pointed out a blue billboard sign that read [Laguna 3km/ Apice 4km]. Jorge and Chavez looked around and realized that they were standing on Volcan Pacaya. The volcano was one of Guatemala's largest and most active volcanos, along with Volcan de Agua and Volcan Acetenango.

"Shit, we've been driving up Pacaya this whole time," said Jorge. He and Chavez were very familiar with Volcan Pacaya.

"Jorge, remember that time we came with your dad. and he split a six-pack with us?" said Chavez.

Jorge laughed and said, "Ahuevos, we were only thirteen. We were drunk by the time we got to the top. My dad got pissed because we wouldn't stop acting like idiots."

Jorge remembered that there was an information center further up the road, but the more they ascended, the more he noticed how empty the area was. There weren't any people in the surrounding villages, and no other cars could be seen on the road. It was like a ghost town.

The car approached the park's ticket booth. It was abandoned as well. No one could be seen anywhere around the vicinity.

"No one is here," said Jorge as he got out of the car to get a better look.

Everyone stepped out of the Lancer to discuss their next move.

"We could go back home," suggested Thomas. He was tired from all the driving. "What about the Laguna? It sounds like a place we can park the car and relax until we decide to go back," suggested Victor.

Jorge pitched a third option with an eager spirit.

"I think we should climb the volcano. I don't know why, but it seems like the right thing to do. After everything that's happened, I don't think the adventure is over. No lying, guys; this is something we have to do. Thomas, I can't let you go home without doing this one last thing."

Thomas didn't actually care what they did. He just wanted to rest for a second. He leaned on the mangled car with both hands tucked into his pocket, assessing the last twenty-four hours. Then he looked at each one of his friends and said,

"I'll do whatever."

Victor walked behind an abandoned facility to find a place where he could urinate. He also needed time to think. His mind was focused on the fact that he had almost been killed. It wasn't easy for Victor to comprehend his fragile existence. He was always aware of the moment, never reflecting on the past nor worrying about the future. After finishing his personal business, he took a seat on an old bench and took a deep breath. There was something comforting about the quiet and empty jungle. It allowed him to regain his composure.

Chavez sat on the trunk of the car and concentrated on two particular things, the UFO and his mortality. He thought of the giant fireball that shone thousands of feet in the night sky. The image had never left his mind. Although he was open to the idea that alien life existed, Chavez wasn't convinced that they had seen an alien spacecraft. It was difficult for him to make sense of what he saw, but he knew how it made him feel. His life was passing by, and there was no more time to waste.

"Guys, Jorge's right. We can't stop now," he unexpectedly said to the others. "We partied all over the city, got in a fight, got kicked out of a strip club, went to a rave, saw some kind of UFO, and almost got killed. I don't know about you, but I'm not ready to go home. I think we should climb this volcano. I also think it's something we're supposed to do," said Chavez.

"Shit, Geoffrey, what the fuck happened to you in San Pedro? I've never seen you this pensive," said Jorge, who rarely used Chavez's first name.

"Life is short, and we shouldn't waste any time. There is a reason we came here, and we have to take advantage of that," he told the others, who were a bit shocked by his uncharacteristically deep sincerity.

Sara sat by herself next to the ticket booth, smoking a joint to calm her nerves. She was grateful to be alive. She was grateful to Thomas for saving her life. The sound of the gunshots was still fresh in her mind. It left her hands white and still shaking. At the moment, the sight of Thomas was the only thing calming her nerves.

Jorge walked over because he knew that she was still uneasy.

"Hey, what about me?" he asked. Sara blew smoke in his face before he snatched the joint from her.

"Are you okay?" he asked his cousin.

"Yeah. I'm glad we're all okay," she replied with a smile across her face.

"I was afraid that you were going to show up crying at your house. The old men would be pissed if they found out what happened," reminded Jorge. He referred to his father and uncle, Sara's father.

"I wasn't crying," denied Sara.

"Don't give me that shit, Sara. I know what I saw," said Jorge patronizingly. He rubbed his right index finger under her chin to let her know he was only kidding. Something about his comfort allowed her to finally release the emotions she held. She cried, and Jorge consoled her.

"Thank you, Jorge," she said before giving him a kiss on the cheek.

"So, what the fuck, guys? What are we going to do?" asked Thomas.

"I don't know, what do you think, Jorge?" asked Sara.

"Well, this is what I propose. I think that these people are on some community retreat or protest in the city. We should take advantage of that and go to the volcano top for free." His words were met with silence from the others. They were still processing everything. "Thomas, you have no idea how incredible this shit is. Once you get to the top, you're going to thank me."

Thomas just lowered his head and laughed. By that point, the adventure was too unbelievable to be true. "Why stop now? Lead the way, Jorge," he said.

"Let the adventure continue. What else could happen to us?" said Victor.

"Ahuevos, what are we waiting for?" added Chavez.

They finished the joint, got back into the Lancer, and drove towards the top, as far as the road would lead them. The car scattered dense dirt clouds in the air the entire way up. Thomas looked straight down from his window and cringed after noticing that only a couple of feet separated the car from the edge of the road.

Volcan de Agua, Guatemala's largest volcano, rose from the horizon. It was enormous.

"That's more than twice the size of Pacaya. It takes two days to get to the top," said Jorge.

"It looks cold up there," mentioned Thomas as he noticed the ice caps at the top.

They arrived at an empty lot. "This is where we can park, pull in," said Jorge. It was empty. There weren't any poor locals directing traffic or innocent children offering services for a morsel of charity. Such services allowed the locals to earn tips as the government continued to exploit their land.

Just as Thomas was ready to park, Jorge remembered that there was another parking lot that was closer to the crater. "You know what? Turn around and keep driving. This is the wrong parking lot. It's not the one I remember."

Thomas did as he was instructed. It didn't take long for them to find the second parking lot. It was located where the volcano trail started.

"There it is, on the left," said Jorge.

Thomas drove down a narrow path that led to the lot that was surrounded by crumbling homes made of metal sheets and sticks. He pulled into the empty welcome center. The wind was the only thing that was welcoming them. The food stands and souvenir shops were there, but not a soul other than them.

Everyone got out of the car to stretch before the rigorous climb. Thomas didn't think it was necessary. He expected a challenging task, but he also thought his years of physical training would carry him the entire way to the apex. He felt this way despite having taken graduate-level physiology and knowing the mechanics of gas exchange. He was from a place that was below sea level, where atmospheric oxygen pressure was higher. At high altitudes, there wasn't enough pressure or oxygen to meet his requirements.

Jorge took one of Thomas' book bags and filled it up with the essentials: his weed, a pipe, a few warm cans of beer, their cell phones, and their wallets. Thomas grabbed another sports bag and filled it with the two cans of refried frijoles, a loaf of bread, and a bottle of chardonnay he had taken from a cousin's wedding.

"How long do you think it will take?" he asked.

"About 45 minutes; the idea is to get a steady pace and control your breathing. The air gets thinner the higher you go," replied Jorge. Thomas and Sara would soon realize exactly what Jorge meant.

Jorge brought everyone to where the path started. They stood side by side, gazing at the challenge at hand. The first thing Thomas noticed was that it was steep, very steep. Still, he was delusional in thinking that weight training was going to be beneficial.

"Is it paved with rocks the entire way?" asked Thomas.

"No, it's just like this at the beginning. The rest of the way is just dirt and jungle," replied Jorge.

Jorge wasn't concerned about the arduous climb. He was more concerned that the place was so empty. It created a sense of uneasiness among the peace.

"Let's finish this adventure," he said to the others. It was their moment to culminate what had happened over the last twenty-four hours.

Everyone struggled for the first fifty meters. Thomas immediately noticed his struggle to breathe. His strength was quickly getting weaker. Sara was in the worst shape. She didn't have the physical strength nor the lung capacity to keep up with the others.

"This is the hardest part," said Jorge as he noticed everyone struggling to adjust.

The remainder of a tree-covered path led directly to the volcano's ash land. Once they got there, it would be an additional twenty-minute hike to the crater.

"I appreciate this, Jorge. If I don't come back to Guate, at least I can say that I climbed Pacaya," gasped Thomas.

"Don't worry about it, man. These last two years have been the most fun of my life. But this is only the beginning. We're going to look back on these days when we're older with families and laugh at all the crazy things we did," said Jorge.

He appreciated Thomas's friendship. Often, their antics allowed Jorge to forget about the suffering that had engulfed his soul when his parents divorced. Thomas unknowingly entered Jorge's life at a very crucial time. It wasn't a coincidence that their paths crossed. God, Life, or some other metaphysical force brought them together to help one another during the frightening years of the quarter-life crisis.

Victor, Chavez, and Jorge walked a few meters ahead of Thomas and Sara, who decided to team up to help one another. The path wound vertically at a thirty-degree angle the entire way. The land was fertile with rich soil and bounteous brush. The rocks and dirt slid underneath their shoes after every step. They all had to keep a strong balance to avoid painful consequences.

Sara's small frame and powerless legs couldn't bear the intensity of the climb. Thomas was further ahead of her, struggling nearly just as much. As he would stop to wait for Sara, the others would continue at their pace.

"C'mon Sara, we have to keep going," said Thomas as he grabbed her hand.

"I don't know if I'm going to be able to finish this, Thomas. I shouldn't have smoked that last joint," she said.

Thomas laughed and said, "Me too."

Jorge, Victor, and Chavez eventually stopped at an abandoned outhouse to wait for Thomas and Sara. They used the time to regain their energy and enjoy the view. The world seemed so small from that viewpoint. Victor noticed the highway. He thought the cars looked like fleas zipping along the stretch of road.

Jorge didn't spend much time focusing on the view. He was still concerned at the fact that the park was so empty. The thought that the volcano was about to explode passed through his mind. He began to wonder if everyone evacuated. Instead of wondering and waiting, he preferred to continue with the climb. Eventually, Thomas and Sara dragged their exhausted bodies to the spot and dropped their rear ends to the ground.

"Shit Jorge, I had no idea how hard this was going to be," said Thomas. He and Sara weren't recuperating as fast as the others. Thomas was embarrassed and didn't want to make them wait. "Move ahead, and we'll catch up," he said. The feeling of shock throughout his entire body could only be healed with time. He and Sara needed to rest before they continued.

"Okay, we'll try not to walk as fast. See you at the top," said Jorge.

Thomas and Sara eventually moved forward at their own pace. Sara couldn't help but take the humor out of her poor conditioning. Her limp body wobbled through the pain as she advanced at a turtle's pace.

"I never thought that I was in such bad shape, Thomas. Thanks for staying behind to help me," she said.

"Hey, I'm struggling just as much as you are. If you weren't here, I'd probably be walking this whole thing by myself," said

Thomas. He grabbed her hand and didn't let go until they got to the next rest point, where the others were already waiting.

Jorge and Chavez drank a warm beer to rehydrate. Victor kept admiring the view. This time, he stared out at the grand view of Volcan de Agua. From his viewpoint, the gray-blue earthly protrusion seemed to take up the entire atmosphere. The sky was clear, and he could follow the view all the way to the top.

Jorge walked up next to him only to be engulfed with the same feeling of wonder as Victor. He stared at a colonial-style town at the bottom of the volcano and thought of the people as nothing more than tiny specs in the overall portrait of life. The view made them both feel small and insignificant. It also made them appreciate the grander scheme of things.

"We're only a fraction of something bigger," said Jorge.

Sara and Thomas were busy catching their breaths. They lay down underneath a hut made of straw and wood. Thomas looked up and noticed a large wasps nest hidden in the corner of the roof. He counted six wasps nourishing their larva. Sara noticed, too, and slowly moved to another spot. The movement alerted the wasps. They began to fly around the parameters of the nest, which made Sara and Thomas move away from the hut.

Everyone continued the march upward. It didn't take long for Thomas and Sara to find that they were alone again. They were struggling more than ever to gain ground. Thomas and Sara had become a team of slackers while the others tried to reach the top as quickly as possible. Both were aware of the growing distance, but they no longer cared. They stopped every couple of minutes to catch their breath and laugh about their weak conditioning.

Along the way, they came to an open, grassy plain that Thomas saw as an excellent place to rest. Thomas unloaded his bag and threw his body on the ground. All he could see was the sky, and all he could hear was the ringing sound in his head. Sara could feel the pain leave her legs while the cool grass soothed her neck and back. Their exhausted bodies tried to regain homeostasis.

"I never want to leave this place. Fuck the crater; I think we've walked enough. We should celebrate," gasped Thomas.

He sat up and reached for his bag to get the bottle of chardonnay.

"I think that we both need a drink," said Thomas.

"What's Jorge going to say?" asked Sara. Thomas just looked at her without answering. "Shouldn't we drink that with the others?" Thomas just continued staring. He could care less about drinking it with the others. They both smiled at each other and shrugged their shoulders.

"Salud, Jorgy boy," said Thomas as he raised the bottle to the sky.

"Would you like the first drink?" he offered Sara.

"I think you should go first because you opened it," she

said.

Thomas took a giant chug out of the bottle. Sara watched as chardonnay trickled down his neck and onto his shirt. She wiped his neck with a gentle touch, unable to resist her attraction for him. Thomas did not expect her to do that.

He handed the bottle to Sara, and she also took a long guzzle.

They couldn't help but laugh at the entire situation. It was the first time that they had ever been completely alone with each other. There was nothing holding them back from doing what they had always wanted to do.

"You're always there to help me. Remember the time when you took me home because I got too drunk at Rumba Bar?" asked Sara.

"Yea, I remember how nervous I was," he said.

"Why?" she asked. Although Sara knew. She was just

playing dumb.

"You didn't stop rubbing my thigh in the car," he said.

"My God, I was so drunk. I'm sorry," she said.

"Don't worry. I liked it. I just wasn't sure how to react at the time," he said.

"I've always wanted to talk to you about that night. I mean, I knew what I was doing, and it wasn't like you were taking advantage of me," said Sara.

"I don't know. I was just respecting my boundaries at the time. We had just met, and I wasn't in the position to start pissing people off. But believe me, I regret not making a move," he said.

There was no force on earth that could unlock the attraction between their eyes. Thomas noticed the finest details of her hazel irises while Sara admired the structure of his face. A brief, awkward silence ensued. The sexual tension was high. Both of them wanted the other to make a move. Thomas proceeded to place his hand on top of hers and gently rub between her fingers. It was all that Sara needed to feel a rush overcome her body. Thomas took a final gulp from the chardonnay bottle and passed it to her. She did the same and then put the bottle down.

Thomas leaned forward and gave her a light peck on her lips. They both pulled away a couple of inches to absorb what was happening, and then they kissed again. They kissed lightly as Thomas laid her on the grass. He leaned over her and supported himself and her head with his left elbow. His right hand was placed on her abdomen. It coursed along her hips and moved underneath her shirt. The move caught her by surprise, but she let him continue.

Thomas' fingers slipped through her bra and caressed her silky nipples. Sara couldn't deny the pleasure that she was feeling. Their kissing became more aggressive, and she began to breathe heavier. His hand softly worked its way down her belly. He glided his finger around her naval as she passionately kissed the side of his face. She nearly lost control as his fingers brimmed the skin under her panty line. He slowly dug further and further toward her intimate area. She felt a tickling sensation, which she liked. Once the tips of his fingers rubbed against her clitoris, she grabbed his wrist with both of her hands and stopped kissing. Sara didn't want him to think that the decision to have sex was his. She would be the only one to decide how far things went.

Higher above, Jorge led the way while Victor and Chavez followed behind at a steady pace. After walking non-stop for twenty minutes, they came out from the jungle. They stood at a crossroads underneath the sky. Everyone looked around for a second to assess the location. One path of the fork led upward to the left, and the other led downward to the right, closer to the edge of the volcano. Chavez looked around and noticed that they weren't alone.

"Guys, look!" he said.

There were two workers dangling high in the air from some sort of electric pole. Chavez decided to whistle at them for directions.

"How do we get to the top?"

One of the workers pointed to the top path and yelled, "Left!"

The three adventurers gave a wave of thanks and walked on the left path toward the pinnacle. It wouldn't be long before there was nowhere left to go.

Jorge turned to Chavez and asked, "Do you remember any of this?"

Chavez looked around to find something that sparked his memory, but there was nothing of the sort.

"This shit looks like an atomic bomb went off," he replied while gazing at the dark sky. It was covered in a thick, black haze that was spewing out from the crater. They approached a humungous ash valley about two hundred feet deep. It sloped upward from the bottom until the ash was replaced with hardened, volcanic rock.

They decided to take a rest and wait for Thomas and Sara to catch up. Victor stood along the valley's edge with his hands in his pockets, admiring everything that his eyes could see. Every inch of the view stimulated his senses in an unexplainable way. He was having a moment of reflection upon the last two years that he had spent living with Kayla. They were the best years of his life. He wished that she was there with him, experiencing the new horizon.

"Where the fuck are these people?" asked Jorge out of

frustration. He could see a stream of lava flowing from the volcano and wanted to get closer to it.

"I don't know, but Thomas has been alone with her for a long time," said Victor to instigate Jorge's worries. He trusted Thomas in many ways, just not necessarily to be alone with his younger cousin. To him, they were both a pair of crazy bastards capable of anything with idle time.

Eventually, Sara and Thomas continued their ascension to the top at their own pace. They took their time nursing the overdue romance. The walk didn't seem as exhausting anymore. They were able to enjoy the time, holding hands the entire way up. They would pass the chardonnay back and forth to each other before pausing to kiss every few meters. Sara found everything to be unexpected, but she liked it.

"I'm so glad this happened," said Thomas.

"I thought it never would," she replied.

They approached the crossroad and wondered where to go. Thomas looked around for a clue. Then he heard a whistle from afar. It was the electricians who were still dangling from the electric pole. "Look over there," he said. They were trying to tell Thomas and Sara to turn back.

"Go down!" yelled one of the men. They had just received word over the radio that the volcano was under an eruption watch. Thomas and Sara couldn't understand him.

"What is he saying?" said Thomas.

"I don't know, but who cares? The others are probably sick and tired of waiting for us. We need to catch up," replied Sara. They ignored the electrician and chose the path to the left. It didn't take long for them to find Jorge. He'd started walking back to see if they were okay.

"I thought you'd never make it," said Jorge.

"We stopped a few times. We were tired," slurred Thomas.

Jorge noticed the goofy look on their faces, and he could smell liquor on their breath.

"You're a couple of drunks; that's what you are," said Jorge.

Thomas didn't want to give away any indication of what had happened between him and Sara. For the remaining hundred feet, he avoided holding her hand, walking next to her, or even motivating her. Chavez and Victor welcomed them to the top. They were eating a tortilla with frijoles to regain energy. Sara and Thomas soon did the same.

They all stood under a tree that survived the last eruption. It was a lonely tree with strong roots that hung off the edge of the remaining soil. They were staring at a perilous wasteland of dark ash and white smoke.

"This has got to be the coolest thing that I have ever seen," said Thomas.

"I'm glad we decided to do this," said Sara.

It was a giant valley with an enormous black rock full of lava in the middle of it. No life could be sustained in such a land. The sky looked like purgatory as it was separated by the black fog over the volcano's peak and the clear blue sky over Volcan de Agua.

"Look over there," said Jorge.

Thomas saw the stream of lava flowing down the volcano; it was a distance away but noticeably electrifying. Rocks were falling from the top, clacking and echoing every time they bounced off the ground.

"Puta, Jorge," said Thomas.

"I know, bro," replied Jorge.

Everyone was rested and ready for the remaining part of the hike. Thomas and Jorge stood above the valley, calculating the descent to the bottom and the climb upward to the crater.

"How long do you think it will take us to get there?" asked Victor.

"I don't know. What do you think, Jorge?" said Thomas.

"I'm not sure. This thing wasn't here last time. The last time I came, there were trees everywhere and an easier path to the top. Everything has been blown up since then," said Jorge.

Without warning, Sara ran and grabbed Thomas by the wrist, pulling him down the ash valley. "Let's go, Jorge!" she yelled. Gravity took over and pushed the two toward the bottom. Thomas slid his feet back and forth as if he was wearing skis in order to keep balance. It left a dust cloud in his path that engulfed Sara as she attempted the same maneuver. They raced downward as their shoes filled with ash sand. It was a thrilling experience. Jorge, Chavez, and Victor soon followed.

On the way up, it seemed like the volcano became more active as they got closer to the crater. The sky was completely hidden behind the smoke and dust in the air. Next, the ground rumbled. Everyone planted their feet firmly to keep balance. Once it was over, everyone continued the march with an unbreakable determination to get to the top. The four friends who started the journey together felt entitled to finish. It would mark the moment when they could let go of the past and enter a new future.

Their feet barreled into the ash, putting their calf muscles to work. Jorge didn't race ahead like earlier. This time, he waited for Sara, extending his hand the entire way up until the ash turned into hardened rock. Fortunately, Victor had grabbed walking sticks for everyone before going down the valley. They all made good use of his quick thinking.

They stepped carefully over the black, porous rocks. It didn't take long for the gang to separate by going up different paths. Each individual mind had used the path that best suited their abilities. Thomas looked around for a minute to see if anyone was nearby. Then he noticed smoke rising out from behind an enormous rock. It flew in his direction, and he noticed it had a strong smell. When he investigated the source, all he found was Chavez peeing into a crater.

The urine caused smoke to rise up from the rocks. Thomas didn't know that was possible. He crouched and felt the ground. He could only keep his hand there for a couple of seconds. The heat from the rocks was so powerful that the lower end of his walking stick suddenly caught fire after being wedged between crevices. Thomas stood up to avoid getting burned. He removed the stick and allowed it to cool down in the wind. To humor himself, Thomas decided to pee on a rock and record a video of the phenomenon on his cell phone.

Thomas and Chavez ran into Jorge and Sara before eventually finding Victor. The ground shook a second time. The tremor only lasted a few seconds, but everyone was starting to become concerned. It felt as though the volcano was alive, breathing underneath their feet.

Strong-willed and determined, everyone maintained a consistent pace throughout the skyward march. They came to a stream of fiery lava that was slithering down with radiant colors of yellow, red, and orange. Its outer skin was covered with soot and ash from the cooling wind that blew at high altitudes. They all took a minute to let the lava's energy touch their souls. For Thomas, Jorge, Chavez, and Victor, it marked the pinnacle of the unimaginable adventure that they embarked on together. Twenty-four hours earlier, they were strolling through life, unconscious of the revelations that they were destined to experience. And now, their fears, their worries, and their insecurities didn't carry the same burdensome weight as they once did. Each one of them felt a purpose to live. The time and place when that purpose was meant to occur was a mystery beyond anyone's control. Until that moment arrived, they all had a duty to create a life of appreciation and dedication for the things and people they loved.

"We're here," said Jorge. There was nowhere left to walk. They had gone as far as they could. The remaining distance to the crater was an impassable gorge of boiling rock and lava.

"They have no idea how we ended up here," said Chavez.

"Through our instincts and the grace of God," said

Jorge.

Victor stood tall among the peak and took in a large breath of air to grasp the moment's essence. His eyes gazed out to the world beneath him, and he smiled with joy. Then he pulled out his cell phone to take a few memorable pictures with his friends.

Jorge approached Sara and put his arm around her neck.

"Make sure our dads don't find out where we were," he told her. Sara laughed.

"Are you crazy? I'm going to tell my dad that I spent the night watching movies with my girlfriends from school." Jorge laughed at the notion that her father thought that she was still an innocent little girl.

"I hope my mom didn't call my brother and sister to check in. I'm supposed to be taking care of them," he said.

"Oh. That's right. Where did she go again?" asked Sara.

"She's in New York with her other family," he replied with embarrassment.

"When did she leave?" she asked.

"On Thursday," said Jorge. Her recent departure fueled a rage that he unloaded by having the craziest night of his life.

Without warning, the volcano shot out a column of steam. It was a god-like roar from the pit of the beast. The monster was rising out of its slumber. Everyone flinched and looked up at how high the steam shot into the air. Jorge's premonition became stronger. He was fully convinced that the rock was about to explode. Dense smoke started to rise rapidly from the crater. That was when everyone else realized that something was terribly wrong. Thomas felt his phone ring in his pocket. It was Mercedes. She finally managed to get through.

"Thomas, are you okay? Where have you been? I've been

trying to get a hold of you all day," she asked with concern in her voice.

"I'm out with some friends," he replied.

"I know you're out with your friends, but where?" replied Mercedes. She always had a strong sense of premonition for Thomas. She felt that he was in danger.

"Why do you need to know where I am?" asked Thomas in a rebellious tone.

"Because it's late, you've been out drinking for the last twenty-four hours, and the news is reporting that Pacaya is about to explode. Haven't you felt the tremors?" Thomas couldn't believe what he was hearing. He looked a second time at the amount of smoke flying out of the crater. Then he looked at the lava river that was growing wider by the second.

"I'm driving home from Antigua. I should be there soon," he told her. Thomas didn't want Mercedes to worry, so he lied.

"Just send me a text when you get home," she asked him.

"I will, my love," he replied.

Thomas hung up the phone.

"We have to get the fuck out of here, now. This volcano is about to explode. That was my friend on the phone. She said it's all over the news," he said.

"Yeah, man, something isn't right," agreed Jorge. The others didn't hesitate to start moving back. They knew that the adventure was over, and any prolongation could be deadly. They didn't want to push their luck any further than they already had.

The descent was much easier than the climb. Apart from the uphill walk of the ash valley, it was all downhill. Gravity helped to push them down the volcano without exerting too much energy. They moved fast while trying to avoid slipping.

Another tremor shook the ground. It caused Chavez to fall and land hard on his rear end. Everyone else knelt down to avoid the same outcome. They were at the mercy of the volcano. It could explode at any moment, and there was nothing they could do. The rumbling didn't stop. "Let's get the fuck out of here!" said Jorge. They stood up and ran down as fast as they could.

It only took fifteen minutes to get to the car. The Lancer looked as though it had been through a war. Thomas managed to drive safely down the narrow dirt roads and onto the paved road without a problem. Along the way, there was an indigenous man without shoes walking as fast as he could toward the bottom.

"Should I give him a ride?" asked Thomas to the others.

"Yeah, of course!" replied Jorge.

Thomas pulled over, and others made room.

"Would you like a lift?" asked Thomas. The local indigenous man nodded his head and walked to the car. He was very gracious and appreciative of their kindness.

"Gracias, gracias, muy amable," he said.

"Do you know that the volcano is about to explode?" asked Jorge.

"Yes, my family left last night. But I came back this morning because we forgot my son's asthma medicine. It was a testament to the immense need for health care in the rural villages.

They drove far enough to get a final glimpse of the volcano's peak. Lava was pouring out in steady waves. The pressure grew to an unstable level until the volcano erupted, unleashing massive debris of soot and rock into the air. It looked like the sky was sucking up the explosion and spitting it back out onto the land. Small pebbles of ash rocks started falling from the heavens. Thomas could hear the car's roof getting hammered with dents and scratches.

"My car can't get any worse," said Thomas. Everyone else sunk into their seats while enjoying the natural display of destruction. There was an overall feeling of safety in the ambiance. They had survived the craziest adventure of their lives. It was as real as anything could ever be.

Within a half hour, they were back in Guatemala City. The gentleman they saved asked to be dropped off at a fast-food restaurant in zone three. From there, Thomas jumped on the Periferico and took the exit to San Cristobal.

The ash didn't stop falling. It was piling up in mounds all over the city. The guard gate at the entrance of Jorge and Chavez's neighborhood had been closed because it was completely covered in ash. Jorge got out of his car and pushed up the front gate so that Thomas could enter. As soon as Jorge got back in the car, it started to drizzle.

The car finally arrived at Jorge's house. Thomas parked it inside the garage port, and everyone got out. As soon as Sara got inside, she went to the kitchen to whip something up for the boys to eat. They never asked; she just offered. Jorge and Victor helped as well. They cooked an entire carton of eggs with chorizo, frijoles, and tortillas. Victor buttered French bread and put it to toast in the oven.

Thomas was up in Jorge's room, rolling up a joint while looking at the falling ash through the balcony window. Chavez came out of Jorge's master bathroom and gazed outside the same window. The water combined with the ash and left a thick soot all over the city, on top of cars, the streets, on light posts, everywhere.

"Have you ever seen something like this before?" asked Thomas.

"No, never; I guess this is the biggest volcanic explosion of my lifetime. I mean, this isn't the first time Pacaya erupts, but it's the first time I've seen ash flood the capital."

Thomas saw it as a final gift from Guatemala before he went back to the States. The land was rewarding him for the time he had spent there, learning more about his origins. Guatemala was always a part of him; he just didn't know it until he moved there.

Everyone sat down to a well-deserved meal, breaking bread in celebration of their survival. Hardly a word was spoken as the food was devoured. They were busy savoring their newfound freedom. Only the sound of clinking silverware could be heard until the last drop of food disappeared.

After the meal, Jorge and Thomas stood outside in the carport, talking about the next trip while drinking a beer and smoking a cigarette.

"What's it called?" asked Thomas.

"The ruins of Yaxha. It's located somewhere within the jungles of Peten," replied Jorge.

"I like the idea. Even if I'm not living here, I'll still come back to the party," said Thomas before taking a sip of beer. "I hope that I come back one day to help Guatemala as much as it helped me. Until the next adventure, Palma," said Thomas. The two friends hit their bottlenecks together, marking a friendship that would last well into the future.

"That's right, my friend," said Jorge.

Three gunshots went off in the distance in sequence.

"I never want to hear another gunshot again," said Thomas. He spoke too soon because two more shots went off.

"That's Guatemala, man, unpredictable," said Jorge as he took a drag of his smoke.

They saw a car pull up in front of the house. It honked twice. Sara ran out the door, saying, "I'm going! I'm going!" She gave Jorge a kiss on the cheek. Then she turned to Thomas and kissed him on the side of his lips. "Bye," was all she said. Thomas smiled and saw her get in the car before it drove away.

"Where's she going?" asked Thomas.

"I don't know, probably to get high somewhere," replied Jorge.

Then the time came for the four friends to part ways. Chavez walked out and said his goodbyes. Before leaving, he mentioned something inspiring to Thomas.

"You know, one of us should write a book about everything that happened."

Thomas smiled. "You're right; maybe you should," he said.

It was just a thought, but Chavez knew that the adventure was worth more than anyone could comprehend at the moment. He stepped onto the street and walked to his house, which was only two blocks away. Soon after, Thomas and Victor parted ways with Jorge and drove to the building where they lived.

Maxwell, the security guard, stood outside the building's lobby, drinking his coffee while admiring the natural phenomena of the ash rain. He heard Thoma's car coming home from a mile away. It was a sound that everyone on the block had become accustomed to hearing. The security guard was surprised to see the Lancer in its current condition. Thomas drove down the ramp to the underground parking lot. Another security guard opened the electronic gate and also noticed the car's condition. Thomas pulled into his spot, and the two security guards ran over to see if he was okay.

"Mr. Flores, what happened to you?"

Thomas wasn't in the mood to give an explanation, but he appreciated their concern. "Estoy bien, estoy bien, gracias," said the American in an exhausted tone. He didn't know what he was going to tell his parents, and he wasn't in the mood to start thinking of excuses. Instead, he just wanted to go to sleep and hope to wake up and realize that it was all a dream. If it wasn't a dream, he'd prefer to deal with the reality in the morning.

Thomas gave the men a brief explanation, and then he headed toward the elevator. He pushed number fifteen, and Victor pushed number twelve. They didn't interrupt the silence because there was nothing left to be said. The elevator arrived at Victor's floor, and the two outsiders slapped hands before saying goodbye. Victor did a final flamenco dance as he walked to his apartment. Thomas laughed.

The elevator closed and re-opened on the fifteenth floor.

Thomas stepped out, walked to room 1504, took out his keys, and opened the cherry oak door. He threw himself on his bed and sent Mercedes a text message that said [I'M HOME]. He kicked off his shoes and went to sleep for a long time.

Chapter Eleven
Farewell to the Heart

A week had gone by since Tropical Storm Agatha tore through Guatemala. The violent storm that followed the volcanic explosion caused death and destruction in the capital's surrounding areas. One hundred and fifty people died due to the over-flooded rivers of the mountains. The damage was costly in every way imaginable. In the aftermath of the storm, a gigantic sinkhole opened up in the middle of the city, pulling a three-story building into the earth's core.

Blood, greed, selfishness, and corruption had soiled the land for long enough. It was flowing in the rivers and in the streets. As a result, the land became angry. It wasn't only the violent criminals, the corrupt politicians, or the squatters who were to blame ~ Guatemala's internal disorder came from a lack of accountability from all its citizens.

Thomas stepped out of a taxicab and gave the driver sixty quetzals. He stood on the Ibanez's front porch with his suitcases and backpack. He rang the doorbell and waited for someone to respond. There was a voice from the speaker.

"Who is it?

It was the housekeeper, Sandra.

"It's me, Thomas," he replied. The main door to the house opened, and he could hear her heading his way. She opened the heavy metal door and greeted him.

"Hello Thomas, adelante." He walked into the house, and it

seemed as though no one was home.

"Is anyone here?" he asked.

"I think Mercedes is somewhere around the house, probably in her room," she replied.

"I'm just coming to say goodbye," he said.

"1 know, I wish you well," said Sandra. Thomas didn't expect such a sincere goodbye from her. "Thank you for everything," he told her.

Thomas went upstairs to find Mercedes. He couldn't leave without seeing her face one last time. He looked in the rooms at the top of the stairs to see if anyone was there, but there wasn't. He walked over to Mercedes' room and saw her typing away at the computer while sitting on her bed, pretending that she didn't hear him come into the house.

"Why didn't you come down to open the door; I know you heard me," he asked her.

"Sorry, it's just that I've been trying to finish this assignment for school," she replied while keeping her eyes on the computer.

"When is it due?" asked Thomas as he looked around the room to see if there was anything he forgot to take home.

"Tomorrow," she said with a smile on her face.

"So smart, yet, so lazy," said Thomas.

He leaned over and gave her a kiss on her soft, white cheek. "How are you?" she asked.

"I'm good. I miss my car," he replied.

"Were your parent's mad?" asked Mercedes.

"No, not really; they're just glad I'm safe," replied Thomas.

"We all are. I knew that something was wrong that day. I knew there was something you weren't telling me. I was sitting here in my bed when I saw the news and immediately thought of you. Then I started to get this weird feeling. I didn't like it. I hope you remember to call the next time you disappear," she lectured.

She knew that Thomas wasn't being completely honest about what happened that night. Before she could continue interrogating him, Thomas changed the subject.

"I'm just glad this semester's over," he said while taking a seat on a desk chair.

"Don't change the topic. I want you to tell me everything that you're hiding from that night," demanded

Mercedes, who had yet to unlock her eyes from the computer to look at Thomas.

"No, I'll tell you another day, but not now. Not while you're still young and stupid," he said. She finally looked at him, grabbed a pillow, and threw it at his head.

Thomas looked at her and realized how much he was going to miss their time together. The fact that she couldn't look him in the eyes told Thomas that Mercedes was feeling the same way.

"When do you come back?" she asked in a cuter tone.

"I don't know; everything depends on how my semester went," he told her.

"And how did it go?" she asked before finally looking at him.

She was hoping that he had good news.

"We'll see, but I think I'll be fine. My grades will be posted next week," said Thomas, who was well aware that he probably failed the semester. "I just wanted to come back and see you before I left," he said to her.

"You better have. I don't think that I would forgive you if you left without saying goodbye," said Mercedes.

She got off her bed and walked to the bathroom. Thomas couldn't take his eyes off her. She bent over to pick up a pair of sandals that Thomas had left at the house. He just stared because she was doing it on purpose.

"I thought you were going to forget these. You left them when you got sick," she said.

"I was wondering where I left those," he said.

"What was it that you got?" she asked.

"Hepatitis A," he said. Thomas emphasized the A because he didn't want anyone to think it was the sexually transmitted type-B or drug-induced type-C. Thomas had contracted a liver disease from eating contaminated food. He was bedridden for six weeks. It caused him to miss a total of seven weeks of the semester.

Mercedes sat back on her bed and continued to chat with an online friend. Once again, she focused her eyes on the screen. They sat for a couple of minutes in silence until Thomas got frustrated.

"Alright, I just wanted to say goodbye," he said while standing up as if he was going to leave.

"Wait, wait, wait; I'm sorry, I was telling a boy from school to stop sending me love letters." She reached for his hand and looked at him with her hypnotizing smile.

"Don't leave; I don't want you to leave." Her fingers lightly interlocked with his as she pulled him towards the bed. Thomas couldn't resist her.

"Are you going to say something, or am I going to talk to myself? The taxi guy is coming back in thirty minutes. It's the only time we have left together," he said. Mercedes moved to the other side of the bed.

"Sit with me," she said. As always, he did what she wanted.

Thomas knew how much she depended on his presence for comfort. He was the only one who could ease her worries and struggles.

"I want you to tell me. How did you finish your semester?" asked Mercedes. She desperately wanted to know whether or not he was coming back.

"Okay, truthfully, I'm not sure. I mean, I might have passed all of my courses, I might not have," confessed. Thomas. It was almost impossible to keep a secret from her.

"Aren't you worried?" she asked while changing the channel on the television.

"No, not anymore," he responded. "I gave it everything I had, and if it wasn't enough, then so be it." Thomas' facial expression became more serious as he proclaimed his new outlook. "I don't know what's going to happen tomorrow. One thing I can tell you about last weekend is that I realized I'm not the only one in control of my life. I can study my ass off and still fail because it's not a part of the plan that God has for me. I don't know what my destiny is, but I'm going to find out," he said.

Mercedes didn't feel the same as Thomas. She didn't want him to make a rash decision that he would regret in the future. "Life is what you make of it, Thomas. I don't want you to use God and your shortcomings as an excuse to quit. I know how important it is for you to become a dentist and make your parents proud; even if you say it doesn't matter, I know it does," she said. Mercedes was unusually wise for her age. That's what he loved most about her.

If this was to be their last day together, then Mercedes wanted to say the right words because she loved him dearly. Thomas had already made a final decision about his future plans, but he still wanted to hear what she had to say.

"I understand you. I'm just saying that I'm not worried about anything anymore. I know that as long as I'm alive, I'll use my time to do something great, something I'm meant to do," he said to her.

"You've dedicated so much time and money to this; don't forget that. I know that I'm a lot younger than you, and I may not have as much life experience, but I know that you'll never forgive yourself if you don't finish your goal," said Mercedes. Thomas kept a stubborn look on his face as her words sunk deep into his mind. Mercedes could get into his head like nobody else could.

"All know is that, no matter where I am, I'm going to take the time to figure it out. Remember, there's time for everything, especially to find happiness," he said while looking up at the ceiling. Then she looked at him, understanding the underlying context of his words. She knew their time was ending and wanted to hold him before he left to start the next chapter in his life.

"I'm going to miss you," she said before embracing his arm and resting her head on his shoulder.

Thomas had spent the last two years learning more about life and himself than most people learn over a lifetime. Gradually, he became someone different than when he arrived. His priorities changed as he learned to fend for himself in a place that was unforgiving to anyone incapable of doing so. Thomas took every experience that had occurred in Guatemala and used it to become a man who was confident in his ability to journey through the rest of his life fearlessly.

He looked into Mercedes' brown eyes and felt a sense of gratitude for everything they'd shared, emotionally and physically. He held her in his arms and closed his eyes, wishing that the moment would never end. Thomas rested his cheek on her head and smelled her scent one last time.

"I'm glad we were given these days to be together," he whispered.

"Me too," she replied. Thomas closed his eyes and let the moment take over...

Ladies and gentlemen, we welcome you to your final destination, Miami. The temperature is seventy-nine degrees, with clear skies. The captain would like to thank you for flying American Airways, and we hope that you fly with us again in the near future. Please make sure to keep your seatbelts fastened and remain seated until we have come to a complete stop. Once again, thank you for flying American Airways, America's most trusted airline.

Thomas opened his eyes and saw that he was home. Once the

plane stopped, he grabbed his carry-on bag and walked down the airplane aisle. As he approached the terminal, Thomas stopped, took a deep breath, and walked proudly toward his unknown future.

THE END

About the Author

Fabian Hernandez is an American author. The son of immigrants, he was born in Louisiana and grew up in South Florida. He's earned a Bachelor's degree in Humanities and a Master's degree in Biomedical Sciences. Fabian combines his imagination, his attention to detail, and his love for the English language to create unique and compelling stories.